Best Wishes
Jerry
from Base Brown
& Partners

LOUIS WEBER, C.E.O.
PUBLICATIONS INTERNATIONAL, LTD.
7373 N. Cicero Ave.
Lincolnwood, IL 60646

Permission is never granted for commercial purposes.

Manufactured in Yugoslavia.

ISBN: 0-88176-405-1

Library of Congress Catalog Card Number: 90-61117

EARTH
A PHOTOGRAPHIC JOURNEY

PUBLICATIONS INTERNATIONAL, LTD.

PHOTO CAPTIONS

Front cover: A rocky inlet on the California coast

Back cover: Angel's Window on the rim of the
Grand Canyon

Page 2: A flourishing temperate hardwood forest
in North America

Page 3: Fall foliage in Pisgah National Forest,
North Carolina

Page 5: A quiet beach on the island of
Madagascar in the Indian Ocean

CONTRIBUTING AUTHOR

John Boslough is a science writer whose articles
have appeared in such publications as *National
Geographic, Smithsonian, Psychology Today,* and
Readers Digest. He has been the science editor for
U.S. News & World Report. His recent book
about mathematician Stephen Hawking is
attracting international attention.

CONTENTS

INTRODUCTION

The planets of our solar system are dominated by desert. The entire surface of earth's only satellite, the moon, is utterly arid. The landscape of Mars is an arcticlike desert, while the surfaces of Venus and Mercury are searing plains too hot to support life. There is nothing like the barrenness of these desert worlds to remind us of the loveliness of our home planet.

What makes Earth so special? The answer is surprisingly straightforward; the one thing our planet has in great abundance that is not found in significant quantities anywhere else in our solar system is water. Out of Earth's waters millions of years ago emerged the only life we know of in this solar system or anywhere else. Ever since the first one-cell organism appeared, the planet's life-nourishing environment has been continuously replenished by endlessly circulating water. Water also helps stabilize and maintain the earth's protective atmosphere.

A wave rolling in from an extended journey halfway across the world displays the awesome power that perpetually shapes and reshapes coastlines.

As you go through this book and examine the wonderful photographs of our planet, think about water and what happens or fails to happen in its absence. Earth is unique because it has been able to retain its oceans and spawn a nearly unbelievable array of life. Look around. You will find that almost every natural feature of our planet has been given its shape, its color, its unique textures, or its stark grandeur by the action of water, past or present. Water is responsible for the grandeur of granite piled upon granite in the Himalaya Mountains, the endless rage of the Atlantic Ocean along England's Cornish coast, the ever-changing colors of the Grand Canyon, the intricate and subtle detail of a prairie wildflower, the power of an alpine glacier, the remoteness and serenity of a tropical island, the eerie stillness of everglades, and the magic of a cumulus cloud challenging our imagination.

Mountains rose up when the great plates in the earth's crust collided. They are proof of the relentless geological energy of our planet. Mountains exist in great profusion on every continent with the exception of nearly flat Australia. There are the Rockies, Sierra Nevada, and aging Appalachians in North America; the Andes and peripheral ranges in South America; the jagged, young Alps in Europe, which are the northeast extension of earth's largest mountain system that also takes in the Carpathians and the Caucasus Range, the Atlas Mountains in northern Africa, and the Zagros, Pamirs, Karakoram, and Himalayas in Asia.

Mountains not only affect weather and provide a unique world for specialized plants and animals, but they directly influence us, providing a source of inspiration and awe in what would be a dull world without them. Think of the power of peaks, such as Mount Everest, the world's tallest. It yearly draws climbers from around the globe, who are willing to undergo extreme discomfort and the risk of death for the chance to stand atop its summit for a minute or two of glory.

Volcanoes are a special kind of mountain. Although there are only an estimated five hundred volcanoes on earth, many count among our most legendary summits. These celebrated volcanoes include Japan's mythical Fuji-san; Aconcagua in South America, the world's tallest volcano at almost 23,000 feet; Kilimanjaro in Africa; Mauna Loa in Hawaii, the world's mightiest mountain that rises 30,000 feet from the bed of the Pacific; Vesuvius that caused history's most famous volcanic disaster in A.D. 79; mysterious Thira in the Aegean Sea that erupted in about 1500 B.C., destroying the Minoan civilization on nearby Crete and perhaps creating the myth of Atlantis; and nasty little Mount Saint Helens in southwestern Washington that erupts about once a century.

Most of the earth's volcanoes occur along a belt that encircles the Pacific Ocean. The great volcanoes of South America, including Aconcagua, are on one end, and Krakatoa, which exploded with the energy of millions of atomic bombs in 1882, is on the other end near the island of Java. Like other mountains, volcanoes inspire and mystify us. But they also frighten us because beneath them smolders fire and brimstone that can strike at anytime. Since the fifteenth century, volcanic eruptions have claimed about two hundred thousand lives.

In high alpine regions, great masses of moving ice flow inch by inch over land and down to the sea. These glaciers form and build as more snow falls during the winter than evaporates in the summer. Eventually, the snow compacts into ice that becomes so heavy and thick it begins to move under the pressure of its own enormous weight. The ice on the bottom of a glacier is pressed into dense pellets that act like frozen ball bearings for the great moving mass above.

The power of a moving glacier sculpts the land beneath it, creating such dramatic terrain as cirques (little rounded hollows), drumlins (little round hills), and moraines (rock and other debris deposited in great long piles). Glaciers are readily accessible throughout northern North America and Europe. If you visit one, you might decide to stroll across its surface or ride a snowmobile on it, giving yourself a chance to sense the glacier's awesome power and size.

Icebergs are a product of glacial movement that you are less likely to visit. Few of us have ever seen an iceberg, except in photographs, much less set foot on one. But despite its inherent danger to shipping, an iceberg is a beautiful sight, according to explorers and seafarers who have encountered one. Icebergs have been compared to gigantic floating castles, churches, fairylands, and pyramids. Their startling whiteness is caused by small, closely spaced gas cavities throughout the ice.

Annual layers of built-up ice and snow gleam
in the pale antarctic sunlight, as this massive iceberg
begins its slow journey north toward eventual
meltdown in warmer seas.

Icebergs almost always "calve" from glaciers in Greenland or Antarctica, although a few drop off into the sea from glaciers in Alaska and Scandinavia. The largest icebergs invariably come from Antarctica because the extremely cold temperatures there allow icebergs to break off from glaciers in enormous chunks. Some antarctic icebergs are more than one hundred miles long and as much as forty stories tall. North Atlantic icebergs are rarely larger than three miles long. Another reason for this great disparity in size is the immensity of the antarctic ice cap, which is larger than the United States, Mexico, and Central America combined.

Moving water in a liquid rather than solid state flows through the rivers of the world with even greater force to shape our lives and environment than glaciers. The earliest civilizations appeared along great rivers, the Tigris and Euphrates, the Ganges, and the Yangtze in Asia and the Nile in Africa. But the world's rivers do more than facilitate commerce and agriculture. Rivers have a timeless beauty that speaks directly to the spirit; this is why many rivers are sacred to people with many different kinds of beliefs.

The Nile is the world's longest river and drains a basin of over one million square miles, but this important river is not the world's mightiest river. The Amazon carries more water than the Nile, Mississippi, and Yangtze combined. Nearly as long as the Nile, the Amazon drops more than three miles during its journey from the Andes to the Atlantic Ocean. It nourishes the earth's greatest rain forest, a jungle of more than two million square miles. Although no great

The Colorado River is not one of the world's mightiest rivers, but with slow, patient effort, the Colorado has cut the greatest slice in the crust of our planet's surface, the Grand Canyon.

civilization lies along its banks, the Amazon's significance cannot be overestimated because of its effect on the climate of its basin and the entire world.

Many people agree that the most dramatic parts of a river are the places where water flows over troubled terrain, forming rapids, or where it plunges straight down in waterfalls. These vertical sections of rivers never cease to delight, amaze, and intrigue us with their sheer power, whether it is the feathery plume of Venezuela's Angel Falls, the world's highest at more than three thousand feet, or the mighty Niagara Falls that is only 160 feet high but discharges more than one hundred times as much water.

What is the world's greatest waterfall? You must decide for yourself whether you are more fascinated by height or volume. Many observers contend that the world's most spectacular falls was discovered in central Africa in 1855 by British explorer David Livingstone. While he was trekking along the Zambezi River, he started hearing a mighty roar. After walking another 25 miles, he finally arrived at the source of the noise: a gigantic waterfall more than forty stories high. Like many of Africa's other great falls, including Kalambo and Tugela falls, Victoria Falls was formed as the river carved a steep chasm across a fracture zone in the crust of the earth.

The Caida de San Rafael tumbles magnificently down a vertical section of the Rio Coca in Ecuador, as it makes its way down from the Andes to drain eventually into the Amazon.

Fresh water comes in many forms; none is more tranquil than a mountain lake. Lakes are ubiquitous, occurring almost everywhere on earth though nowhere in such profusion as in Canada, which has nearly half the lakes in the world. Most Canadian lakes were caused by the great ice sheets that covered North America and northern Europe between ten thousand and two and a half million years ago, and gouged out uncounted numbers of depressions in the bedrock. These basins eventually filled with water and became lakes. Another kind of lake was created when the top of a volcano blew off, forming a crater that could hold water.

The world's largest lakes are rarely found in mountain regions. The biggest lakes are briny inland seas, of which the Caspian Sea is the largest. This immense lake, which is about the size of the state of Colorado, is evaporating at a fairly rapid rate and filling with sediment so that eventually it will cease to exist. This cycle is true of most lakes, which are relatively short-lived geological features. Almost as soon as any lake forms, it begins filling with sediments brought in by rivers and streams. Biology works along with geology to destroy the lake. Organic material from vegetation turns shallow lakes into bogs and ultimately into meadows. Fortunately, the geological processes that take away lakes also make new lakes elsewhere.

In the land of lakes, Crane Lake in Voyageurs
National Park, Minnesota, provides a lovely tree-
lined shore and quiet refuge for a wealth of wildlife.

A desert has almost nothing in common with a cool, mountain lake. But these great areas of parched earth have their own peculiarly awesome beauty. These arid or semiarid regions today account for one-third of the earth's surface, and the amount of desert land is increasing steadily. Deserts are caused by climatic patterns that are usually influenced by the earth's topography. Mountain ranges especially affect air movement and patterns of precipitation. The temperature of the air drops as altitude increases, and this colder air cannot hold as much moisture as warm air. So when warm, moist air moves up the windward slope of a mountain range, the air cools and the water vapor it is holding condenses into droplets that fall as rain or snow. By the time the air passes over the highest summits, it has lost most of its moisture, and the leeward side of most mountains is drier than the windward slope.

This common pattern has helped create some of the world's great deserts, many of which lie in the so-called rain shadows of mountain ranges. The Sahara is on the leeward side of the Atlas Mountains; China's vast Takla Makan and Gobi deserts are in the rain shadow of the Himalayas; and the Atacama Desert gets very little rain because of the Andes. In North America the west side of the Cascade Mountains in Washington is wet, while the east side is dry. The western slope of the great spine of North America, the Rocky Mountains, also receives more precipitation than the eastern slope. This is one cause of the barrenness of the Great Plains.

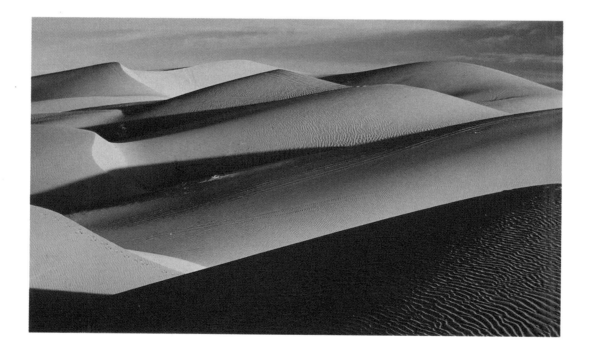

Golden waves of sand in the California Desert retain their shape only for an instant of geological time. This desert is endangered by its proximity to densely populated Los Angeles.

The absence of water is what a desert is all about. But even in an arid region, water can play a significant role. Think of the Grand Canyon. Without the patient work of the Colorado River over millions of years, the canyon would still be filled with the bedrock of a high plateau. Without rivers we wouldn't have enigmatic Zion Canyon, delicate Bryce Canyon, or any of the unique topography that gives the southwestern United States its eerie and timeless beauty. Without water, even the mighty Sahara, the world's greatest expanse of desert, would be just a blank feature on the earth's surface, instead of a land of spires, wadis, scarps, and dry mountains.

The Colorado River and its tributaries have helped shape the Colorado Plateau, which encompasses some of the most spectacular topography in the United States. The plateau offers a unique combination of geology, natural features climate, and human culture. The uplifted layers of rock, gouged out into great canyons, mesas, and buttes over the millennia by rivers, wind, and rain, give the region its essential character.

The barren openness of canyonland and desert contrasts sharply with the lush, dense vegetation of a tropical rain forest. The most spectacularly beautiful of all forested areas, these jungles contain a phenomenal amount of life. As many as one hundred species of trees can live within a single square mile along with a seemingly endless variety of climbing plants, vines, and bromeliads, which live entirely in the upper canopy of the rain forest often fifteen stories above ground. The canopy is also the area where rain-forest animals prowl; all of which are able to fly or climb easily.

Other kinds of wooded area may not be as lush as rain forests, but each has its own unique beauty. Temperate deciduous forests and temperate evergreen forests cover much of North America. Vast boreal forests, consisting usually of just two kinds of trees, such as spruce and fir, sprawl across northern Europe. Forests first appeared three hundred fifty million years ago when enormous mosses and ferns grew up in marshy areas. The first forests that resemble the kind we see today appeared about two million years ago when the earth's climate cooled.

Grassland is one of our planet's major ecosystems, but it is one that has disappeared from much of the world because of cultivation. Large prairies once girdled the globe, from the American Midwest to the great basins stretching from Hungary to Manchuria and south to Australia. Prairies appear almost anywhere it is flat and humid. One of the largest and relatively wild prairies is the Pampa in Argentina, a region of endless tall grass, broken up only by clumps of trees along the banks of rivers and streams.

Grasslands first appeared millions of years ago on bare dry land that had gradually become overgrown with lichens and moss. Prairies were once home to vast hordes of wild animals, such as bison in North America or wild cattle and horses in Europe and Asia. Later, domesticated sheep, cattle, horses, and goats grazed the land, as people began using grasslands for agriculture.

Some grasslands were once wetlands, swamps, and marshes, bursting with life in countless forms. One of the most magical wetlands is Big Cypress Swamp, which extends across southwestern Florida on the periphery of the Everglades. It is a lovely yet inhospitable land of snakes, forbidding thickets, and oppressive heat. You will also find gigantic alligators, deep muck, thick swarms of insects, and bald cypress trees that are more than one hundred feet tall.

A marsh is similar to a swamp, but instead of tall trees covered with moss, a marsh's main vegetation is low-lying grasses and rushes. Many people are unaware of the extent of swamps, marshes, and other wetlands in the United States, none of which is exactly like any other. Wetlands are among the most productive ecosystems anywhere, providing food and shelter for many species of birds and fish, and improving water quality for all life forms by trapping sediments and removing pollution.

Poking through the still mirror of the waters of an Alabama swamp, cypress knees and delicate tall grasses catch the sunlight that filters through the tall old trees.

More than two-thirds of our planet's surface is covered by a single ocean, and the earth is dependent on water for all its unique features from its geology and topography to its climate and amalgamation of life forms. Our integral connection to water makes all of us intrigued by the ocean. People are drawn to those places where sea meets land, creating a mystifying border between two different worlds.

Almost everybody has his or her favorite stretch of coastline. Some people prefer the rocky coast of Maine; others, the jagged cliffs of southern England, the fjords of Norway, the beaches of southern California, the wind and wave battered cliffs of Scotland, the beautiful Dalmatian coast of Yugoslavia with it's great mountains dropping down to the peaceful blue Adriatic, or the awesome headlands of Tierra del Fuego.

On this sea-covered planet of ours, islands hold a special place in everybody's mind. Maybe it is because we all live on an island, whether it is a gigantic continent, such as North America, or a mound of rock in a tropical ocean. Bali in the Indonesian archipelago is one of the most beautiful islands in the world. This

The blue-green waters of the Indian Ocean wash ashore on a beach in the Seychelles, a unique group of about a hundred islands that dot the sea a thousand miles off the coast of Kenya.

island is about the size of the state of Delaware, but it has long beguiled visitors with golden sunsets, sandy beaches, and unfolding layers of terraced rice paddies on the sides of towering volcanoes.

On Bali, as on other tropical islands, we seem to feel the magic of islands more than elsewhere. We feel somehow protected and isolated from the cares of our day-to-day lives by frontiers that are created by nature rather than people. This may help explain why island inhabitants seem to be molded by them, whether it is a tropical paradise surrounded by blue lagoons or a rugged heap of rocks off the coast of Scotland.

Like the coast that separates an island from the rest of the world or the sunset that divides day from night, the edges of things hold an immense attraction. The greatest visual edge of all and a constant in everybody's life is the horizon. Sometimes close and sometimes far, the horizon always separates the known from the unknown, your own world from the next. The sky, the wonderful blue canopy above us all, is the single constant in all horizons.

Scientists believe that Mars and Venus, the two planets nearest us in our solar system, may once have had brief lush periods before succumbing to the desert that is our solar system's most dominant landform. Today, our deserts are the places on Earth that are most like the other planets. Scientists warn us that earth's deserts are spreading at an alarming rate largely because of people. Of all places, the desert draws our attention to the ongoing miracle of life elsewhere on earth in the seas, mountains, valleys, and prairies. By showing us what happens in its absence, the desert reminds us of the beauty and vibrancy of the world that is brought to life by water.

The eighteenth century French philosopher Françoisé Rene, Vicomte de Chateaubriand, said that the forests came before man, the deserts afterwards. Today, people are turning more and more of our planet's landscape into desert. The industrial nations loft fumes into the atmosphere in such volume that it could eventually overheat, turning the earth into a desert world like Venus. At the same time, developing nations in Africa, South America, and Asia are consuming trees at an unbelievable rate, creating hundreds of acres of new desert each day. The total area of the planet now threatening to become desert is fourteen and a half million square miles; that is an area nearly four times as large as the United States including Alaska.

In many ways, the problem of desertification symbolizes our often confused and troubled relationship with our planet. This relationship can be summarized with the question: Should we work to exploit the earth or to preserve it? The answer seems obvious, but people certainly have different ideas when it comes putting this philosophy into action. Whatever becomes of our planet, the choice is ours.

The marvelous pictures in this book show us the great beauty of our world—the mountains, forests, grasslands, wetlands, and deserts. Contrasting with the serenity of the landscape, other pictures show us the grand disorder of clouds, the momentary chaos of a storm, and the glowing brevity of a sunset. But these pictures not only present the great beauty that delights us almost everywhere. The photographs in this book also give us a renewed recognition of how much we humans are children of this earth, how much we love it, and how much we need to guard it wisely, because Earth, our beautiful planet, is our only planet.

Blotting out the sun, the mighty evergreen trees of the Hoh Rain Forest in Olympic National Park in Washington create a wet, dank world below.

MAJESTIC HEIGHTS

The first view of the Teton Mountains is unforgettable. From their base on the floor of the valley called Jackson Hole, the mountains rise almost perpendicularly a mile and a half into the azure blue sky of northwest Wyoming. Surrounded by an array of lesser spires and pinnacles, the tallest peak in the range, Grand Teton, can look like the steeple of a gothic cathedral glistening in the sun. On stormy winter days with dark, mean clouds swirling around the summits and mist drifting up the canyons, the Tetons look like they are slow dancing in the hall of the mountain king.

The Tetons more than satisfy the definition of a mountain: any landform that rises prominently above its geological surroundings. This definition also easily fits the rest of the Rockies along with the great peaks of the Himalayas, the Alps, and the Andes. But smaller geological features that have far less visual impact also qualify. The Ouachita Mountains of Arkansas and Oklahoma are mountains even though they are shorter than the Black Hills of South Dakota. The Appalachians in the eastern part of United States and the fells in England's Lake District are also mountains. In the United Kingdom, where definitions are taken seriously, any hill more than 620 meters (2,046 feet) above sea level is considered to be a mountain. But putting definitions and measurements aside, everybody knows a mountain when he or she sees one.

One reason for this instant recognition is that any mountain worthy of the name carries with it a certain mystique that seems to fit its own particular locale and geometry. Grand Teton and its consort peaks have become an icon of the American West, familiar to all of us from television commercials and movies. Other mountains have also become icons. More than twice the height of Grand Teton, Mount Everest, the world's greatest peak, instantly brings to mind a sense of inaccessibility, discomfort, cold, and danger. Think of Mount McKinley, or Denali, and you immediately imagine Alaska—bold, wild, and arctic. The Matterhorn, which rises from the flatland almost as abruptly as Grand Teton, symbolizes the European Alps, strikingly beautiful yet somehow also very civilized.

Great mountain ranges appear in profusion on every continent except Australia, and even it has a pint-sized system called the Snowy Range. These grand peaks are testimony to the restless geological energy of our planet. For centuries people believed that mountains had simply existed as they were for all time. But

Clouds swirl around the summits of the snow-covered Tetons as the trees in the Bridget-Teton National Forest begin to display their glorious fall colors.

CHAPTER ONE

during the eighteenth century, scientists began to realize that the earth's crust was in constant motion. It moves slowly, and its motion is not apparent, but the earth's surface is constantly moving. In about 1960, geologists began to develop a theory to explain the way in which mountains are formed. Called plate tectonics, this theory maintains that the earth's crust consists of seven enormous, rigid plates that are in constant motion relative to one another, providing a free ride for the oceans and continents on top of them.

Most major mountain building takes place where these giant plates crunch and grind against each other in their slow waltz around the earth. The Tetons, along with the Wasatch Range in Utah, the Sierra Nevada in California, and the Harz Mountains in Germany, formed when huge blocks of the earth's crust were thrust up or tilted along a fracture between moving plates.

In the case of the Tetons, the western block rose and the eastern block sank to form the valley of Jackson Hole. At first there were no mountains on the western side of the valley, just a monolithic forty-mile-long solid block of rock with a precipitous eastern slope. Then glaciers and running water began to erode the rock, sculpturing deep U-shaped canyons and leaving sharp, horn-shaped peaks. This splitting action, followed by wind erosion, accounts for the Teton's abrupt and dramatic eastern slope. Other ranges, notably the Appalachian Mountains and the Alps, were created in a single great uplift when two plates met head on and their leading edges rose up and crumpled all at once.

Our planet's mightiest mountain system that extends more than seven thousand miles and takes in the Alps, the Carpathians, and the Caucasus Range in Europe, the Atlas Mountains in northern Africa, and the Zagros, Pamir, Karakoram, and Himalaya mountains in Asia, mutely attests to the relentless power of geology in constant motion. Geologists believe these mountains formed along the lines where four of the gigantic plates collide. In fact, they are still forming as the frequency of earthquakes in the region attests.

Soaring high above what might otherwise be a flat, dull world, mountains change our weather and climate, provide a specialized environment for animals and plants, and create political and cultural barriers. Because mountains are created by such fierce geologic processes, they bring valuable minerals near the surface where they can be mined. The impact of mountains on our world is important, but in the end, it is the mountains themselves that get our full attention. We go to the mountains to hunt, hike, climb, ski, camp, and breathe the fresh air, or best of all, simply to admire the view.

The Alps are a truly international mountain range,
covering most of Switzerland as well as parts of
France, Germany, Austria, Italy, and Yugoslavia.

CHAPTER ONE

21

A southern extension of the mighty Alps, the
moody and temperamental Dolomites in
northeastern Italy are some of Europe's most
rugged and inaccessible mountains.

CHAPTER ONE

*The moon haunts the sky above a lonely alpine
meadow on Deer Ridge at twelve thousand feet in
Rocky Mountain National Park, Colorado.*

CHAPTER ONE

Startling pinnacles and spires create an otherworldly landscape along the River Li near Guilin in south-central China.

PRECEDING PAGES
The stark beauty of the Rocky Mountains in Glacier National Park, Montana, near the continental divide, contrasts with the smooth tranquility of Lake Saint Mary.

CHAPTER ONE

*Basking in moonlight, peaks of the
Karakoram Range of the Himalayas rise
nearly five miles above sea level.*

CHAPTER ONE

27

*This carnivorous plant, living in Alaska's
Lake Clark National Park, is one of the alpine
tundra's many surprises. Its sticky tentacles are
designed to capture and hold insects.*

OPPOSITE
*Wildflowers brighten the landscape of Arthur's Pass
in the Southern Alps in New Zealand, an
area known for its craggy landscape and
forbidding glaciers.*

LIFE IN THE ALPINE WORLD

Almost no living things have adapted to the bitter cold and ceaseless wind of the summit areas of the highest snowcapped mountains—unless you believe in Yeti, the legendary half-beast/half-man of the Himalayas. But just below the snowfields and above the highest trees, a fragile world of alpine tundra supports a surprising array of life.

The environment challenges the survival of plants and animals with extremes of temperature, a short growing season, high winds, frequent drought, and poor soil. Plants, such as juniper shrubs, mosses, alpine grasses, and lichens, survive by adapting. They use such techniques as dwarfism and matting to keep themselves snuggled low to the ground where conditions are less severe than they are just a foot higher up. Alpine plants also tend to have unusually large root systems and warmth-producing red pigments that make some of these plants appear brown in color.

Animals tend to adapt to subalpine and alpine rigors by modifying their behavior rather than their structure. There are some exceptions, such as flightless grasshoppers and pikas (tiny rabbits with fur-covered feet that inhabit the high Rockies). In the summer a pika builds a miniature haystack of mountain grasses to shelter it from the cold. The yellowbelly marmot stores fat rather than grass; its chubby little body is able to pass a high-mountain winter in hibernation. During the summer surprising numbers of spiders wander alpine snowfields to feed on cold, sluggish insects that have been blown up from below.

The biggest mammals of the high mountain realm are sure-footed mountain goats and sheep. Count yourself lucky if you see a bighorn mountain sheep; these wary creatures stick together in little bands and feed on alpine shrubs and moss. A male has great horns that curve down and back. His body is covered with thick, tannish-gray hair. He might weigh three hundred pounds, but he can scamper up and down nearly vertical cliffs more nimbly than the most skilled human climber because his specialized footpads grip rock more surely than the best hiking boots.

Mount Everest glimmers in bright sunlight with the Khumbu Glacier curled at its feet.

TALLEST MOUNTAIN

In 1852 a British clerk who had been studying charts and maps in the Office of the Survey of India looked up and announced to his supervisor: "Sir, I have discovered the world's tallest mountain."

Even though this peak is a geologically young mountain, it had not suddenly sprung into existence, as the clerk's comment suggests. This mountain had already stood on what is now the border between Tibet and Nepal for a few million years before human beings appeared on earth. But until that moment in 1852, the 29,028-foot-tall mountain, then called Peak XV, had not been recognized as being among the world's tallest summits. In those days the tallest peak was believed to be a mountain now called K2 in the Karakoram sub-range of the Himalayas. It is 28,250 feet tall.

In 1852 Europeans did not known that the newly discovered peak already had a Tibetan name, Chomolungma, which means "goddess mother of the world." Soon after additional computations were made confirming the clerk's calculations, the peak was named in honor of Sir George Everest, an early Sur-veyor General of India. No Europeans had seen the mountain; it had been discovered, measured, and named from a distance. A Western exploratory expedi-tion didn't get near the base of the peak until the 1920s. No one made it to the summit until 1953.

Now, more than four decades after the British gave up their Empire on the Indian subcontinent, some mountaineers and geographic authorities believe it would be appropriate to restore the original Tibetan name to the earth's mightiest mountain. But the peak's English name is so ingrained in our imaginations that it does not seem likely that the mountain will have its name restored anytime soon.

*In Tibetan the mountain is called Chomolungma,
the "goddess mother of the world." We know it as
Mount Everest, the tallest mountain on earth at
29,028 feet.*

CHAPTER ONE

CHAPTER ONE

32

Reflected in an alpine tarn, the Matterhorn in the Pennine Alps on the Swiss-Italian border is about 14,700 feet tall. Its sharp peak speaks of the mountain's comparative youth.

One of the most photogenic mountains in the world, the lovely Matterhorn, rises arrogantly into the sky more than a mile above sea level near Zermatt, Switzerland.

FIRE FROM BELOW

Mount Fuji is a mountain among mountains. It is an astonishing sight from almost any angle, even when its summit is hidden by the clouds that seem to be drawn to it by the same force that brings an estimated fifty thousand pilgrims to the mountain every year. Fuji-san, as it is called by the Japanese who consider it a sacred mountain, is hypnotically alluring. The tallest mountain in Japan at 12,389 feet, its beauty and nearly symmetrical cone have inspired Japanese poets, painters, and potters for centuries.

According to legend, an earthquake brought Fuji-san into existence in 286 B.C. But the mountain is actually a volcano that was created by a series of eruptions over many centuries. Its last major eruption was in 1707. Volcanoes, such as Fujiyama, are a special breed of mountain. Like other mountains, they mystify us, inspire dreams of conquests not yet achieved, and make our spirits soar. But volcanoes also have another dimension. Beneath their serene snow-capped peaks smolders the fire of potential destruction and death.

Since the fifteenth century, volcanic eruptions have claimed an estimated two hundred thousand lives. Volcanoes caused such terrible disasters throughout history that these smoldering mountains came to play a role in some religions. The Romans attributed the power of volcanoes to Vulcan, their god of fire whose name eventually led to the word *volcano*. They suffered one of history's most famous volcanic disasters when Vesuvius erupted in A.D. 79 and destroyed the towns of Herculaneum, Pompeii, and Stabiae.

A volcano occurs at an aperture in the earth's crust where hot gases, rock fragments, and lava burst through the surface. Technically, a volcano is any such vent in the earth's surface, including a fumarole or geyser, but most of us think of a volcano as a mountain. These volcanic mountains can build up quickly from ash, cinder, and lava. In Mexico in 1943, a beginning volcano, now called Parícutin, built a cinder cone that was more than five hundred feet high in less than a week.

There are about five hundred volcanoes on earth, but the mystique of these mountains exceeds their number. Volcanologists have identified a number of extinct volcanoes, such as Kilimanjaro in Tanzania. If a volcano is described as being extinct, it has not erupted during recorded history and is not expected to

The incredible beauty of Fujiyama's snow-capped
cone, ringed with lakes and pine forests, has inspired
painters, poets, and religious thinkers for centuries.

erupt again. The ever-present danger of eruption probably accounts for the fact that a disproportionate number of volcanoes are among our planet's most famous mountains. Aconcagua is the world's highest volcano and the western hemisphere's tallest peak at 22,831; it is now considered extinct. Thira, a volcano in the Aegean Sea, erupted in about 1500 B.C., probably destroying the Minoan civilization on nearby Crete and perhaps inspiring the legend of Atlantis. Mauna Loa in Hawaii is the world's largest mountain, rising about thirty thousand feet from the floor of the Pacific Ocean with a base sixty miles wide.

Predicting when an eruption may occur is an uncertain business, since most volcanoes do not announce their timetables in advance. Volcanologists who measure the buildup of pressure inside a volcanic cone use an instrument that sounds like it comes from a pinball parlor: A tiltmeter measures the expanding surface as gases heat and expand inside the mountain. Volcanologists also take seismographic readings because small earthquakes frequently accompany an impending eruption. A few volcanoes, especially those in Hawaii, have a built-in warning mechanism: Before an eruption, the temperature of the surrounding area rises noticeably and clouds of gas pour from the volcano's vent.

Most volcanoes occur along the boundaries of the same immense plates that create mountains and other geological features. A volcano is most likely to appear where two plates collide and one of the plates is forced under the other. As the two plates rub together, they generate an enormous amount of friction that melts some of the crust material. This melted material rises as magma, and when it reaches the surface, it creates a volcano. One can also appear when two plates spread apart, allowing molten material from deep within the earth to flow toward the surface. This phenomenon usually occurs on the ocean floor where rising magma creates an underwater mountain range. The immense Mid-Atlantic Ridge, which rises above the ocean's surface at Iceland and other volcanic islands, was created in this way.

Volcanoes never cease to fascinate and frighten us. The immense power and spectacle of a volcanic eruption provide a window to our planet's ever-changing, ever-mystifying interior. We never know when these geological forces will come into play, spreading a swath of lava and ash that can smother a forest or a town and claim a thousand lives in an instant.

The plume of superheated water and steam, shooting above the trees from this geyser in Yellowstone National Park, was heated by the same fire deep within the earth that causes other volcanic activity.

CHAPTER TWO

*This land of smoke and fire, White Island near
the coast of New Zealand, is a sea-floor volcano.
The island is being created by almost constant
eruptions of the volcano.*

CHAPTER TWO

The serenity of this volcanic island belies the fact
that it erupted as recently as 1988. Volcanoes also
formed the other Banda Islands that are part of the
Republic of Indonesia.

CHAPTER TWO

*At Volcanoes National Park in Hawaii, lava and
ash create an otherworldly landscape where
vegetation found in other parts of the islands
seems out of place.*

*PRECEDING PAGES
Mount Kilamanjaro is the highest mountain in
Africa. This extinct volcano rises in two snow-
capped peaks that are joined by a broad saddle of
volcanic ash and rock.*

*Hotter than any fire that burns on earth's surface,
incredible friction below the earth's fragile crust
melts rock into magma and sends it spurting to the
surface, where it is known as lava.*

CHAPTER TWO

44

Disguised with a cloak of green, these volcanic peaks of Moora Island are part of an intensely active belt of volcanoes that encircles the Pacific Ocean from South America to the Indonesian archipelago.

OPPOSITE
The crater of Haleakala on Maui, Hawaii, is an arid wasteland that contrasts sharply with the green fields and forests that surround the base of this large volcanic mountain.

RING OF FIRE

More than a century after it erupted in an almost unbelievably violent blast, people still shudder when they hear the name Krakatoa. This volcanic island used to rise about three thousand feet above sea level in the Selat Strait between Java and Sumatra. But in 1882 Krakatoa was torn apart in an explosion that released more energy than six million atomic bombs. The blast was so great that it was heard three thousand miles away. So much ash, rock, and lava were emitted that new islands were formed and debris was scattered across the entire Indian Ocean. The ensuing tsunami that had waves 130 feet high caused death and destruction hundreds of miles away.

Along with Krakatoa, most other volcanoes on Earth are found on an enormous belt that almost entirely encircles the Pacific Ocean. Called the Ring of Fire by volcanologists, it occurs along the edges of the great Pacific plate. According to the theory of plate tectonics, volcanoes arise where this plate, moving as much as four inches a year, grinds up against or separates from the continental plates that make up North and South America, Asia and Indonesia, and Australia.

The volcanoes along the Ring of Fire extend from Aconcagua in the southern part of South America along the coast and into North America through Mexico. Mount Saint Helens is just one of a series of volcanic peaks known as the Cascades that extend for about seven hundred miles from Lassen Peak in California to Mount Garibaldi in British Columbia. The ring continues north through southern Alaska, then down the eastern coast of the Soviet Union, through Japan to Indonesia. Krakatoa is its southeastern terminus.

With each new eruption, Mount Saint Helens transforms itself into a different mountain. The steep cone with which people in this century had been familiar has become a pronounced crater.

MOUNT SAINT HELENS

Sometimes referred to as the American Mount Fuji because of its classic conical shape, Mount Saint Helens, which is about forty miles from Portland, Oregon, in southwestern Washington, is called Tah-one-lat-clah by the Klickitat Indians. The name means "fire mountain." In 1792 Captain George Vancouver gave the volcano an English name in honor of Lord Saint Helens, who was Britain's ambassador to Spain. Geologists believe the current mountain was built up over the last one thousand years on top of the remains of an ancient volcano. Mount Saint Helens has a history of erupting every 100 to 150 years. The last eruption before this century occurred in 1857.

Following a series of earthquakes that began in March 1980, gases inside the mountain reached a critical pressure then exploded outward. The eruption blew 1,300 feet off the top of the mountain and propelled thousands of tons of fine ash, rock, and debris 12 miles into the sky. Thousands of acres of Douglas fir were leveled, and mud and debris from the eruption filled valleys, lakes, and rivers. Vast numbers of birds, animals, and fish were killed along with 57 people. Hot ash and rocks from the eruption started forest fires and melted snow, and the resulting floods and mud slides washed away buildings, roads, and bridges.

The eruption also spread a thick layer of volcanic ash over a large area, destroying crops and blanketing cities. Pulverized rock and ash debris in the atmosphere created dramatic sunsets around the world for weeks. The eruption was so sudden and violent that nobody old enough then to understand what happened is ever likely to forget it. Geologists anticipate that Mount Saint Helens will erupt again in another hundred years.

*In a burst of terrifying beauty, Mount Saint Helens
in the Cascade Range erupts with devastating force
once every century. This eruption in March 1980
blew debris 12 miles into the sky.*

CHAPTER TWO

*New plants struggle to get a foothold in this field of
corded lava rock, which is also known as pahoehoe,
in Volcanoes National Park, Hawaii.*

*Mount Ngaurone billows forth a deadly cloud of
fine volcanic ash and superheated steam. The
volcano's steep-sided cone has been built up by
many similar eruptions.*

CHAPTER TWO

FROZEN GRANDEUR

The Matthes Glacier winds its way through a valley in the mountains of Alaska's Boundary Ranges like a gigantic white road. From a distance it looks smooth enough to drive down. More than sixty miles long, the ice field is surrounded by the jagged ramparts of its peripheral peaks. Like all glaciers, the Matthes moves very slowly, but not so slowly that it prevents the scientists who have been studying the glacier for more than thirty years from gathering a wealth of information about its movement as well as new knowledge about its mountain environment.

Studying the Matthes Glacier helps scientists learn about short-term climatic changes. They hope they will find answers to some of the big environmental questions of our time, such as whether global warming is really taking place or whether another ice age is on the way. Experts around the world agree that studying glaciers over a long period of time is one of the best ways to pursue the answers to these questions.

Glaciers are huge masses of ice that flow slowly over land. They form in polar regions and in high mountain valleys when more snow falls during the winter than melts and evaporates during the summer. As the snow builds up in layers—one for each winter—its ever-heavier weight causes snow beneath the surface to compact into tiny grainlike pellets, which are eventually pressed into dense crystals of ice. Over time, the ice becomes so heavy and thick, sometimes nearly two miles in depth, that it begins to move under the pressure of its own enormous weight.

Along with examining these yearly layers, which give them information about weather and climatic changes, scientists also measure the rate at which a glacier flows. Gravity invariably pulls glaciers downhill, with the compacted ice crystals deep below the surface gliding over one another and allowing the entire mass of ice to move. If you have ever strolled across a glacier, you undoubtedly found the surface stiff and rigid. But the mass of ice below your feet is in constant motion and often splits into sections and forms enormous cracks called crevasses. When the glacier flows over uneven or especially steep terrain, crevasses are most likely to form. Depending on the local topography, the surface of a glacier almost always moves more swiftly than the compressed ice below. This accounts for further cracking and splitting.

A moving glacier possesses nearly unbelievable power to shape and sculpt the terrain over which it slowly glides. An advancing ice mass can scoop up fragments of rocks and drag them along its base, grinding the bedrock below to a polished, although occasionally scratched, surface. Near the peaks of such mountains as the Tetons in Wyoming, you can walk into a cirque, another kind of remnant left by a long-gone glacier. This rounded hollow was produced when the upper section of the moving ice pulled down immense chunks of rock from surrounding cliffs. If

*Prongs of ice sprout from Mendenhall Glacier in
Alaska. Glaciers collect a layer of fresh snow each
winter, in which scientists can find a record of
weather and climate.*

CHAPTER THREE

you hike in the Rockies and Sierras, you may have to scramble over a moraine. This ridge of rock, clay, and sand was deposited by a glacier along its side or at its bottom end. The names of some of the other land forms created by glaciers sound like they come from the Brothers Grimm. *Drumlins* are oval-shaped hills consisting of rock debris, and *eskers* are long, narrow ridges of sand and gravel deposited by water flowing in a tunnel beneath a melting glacier.

Photographs can only glimpse but never capture the power and grandeur of these moving sheets of ice. To experience the majesty and power of a sea of ice that seems almost alive, you should go to see one for yourself. There are more than twelve hundred glaciers in Europe, the best known are the glacier on Mont Blanc in the French Alps and the Aletsch Glacier near the Jungfrau in the Swiss Alps. The Jostedal Glacier in Norway, covering about three hundred square miles, is the continent's largest. Glaciers also flow in great profusion in the northwestern part of North America. The largest and probably the most famous is the Malaspina Glacier. It is about 840 square miles of moving snow and ice on Yakutat Bay in Alaska.

You can visit other glaciers in Banff National Park in Alberta. Glacier National Park in Montana has about fifty glaciers. There are several small glaciers on Mount Rainier in Washington, and elsewhere in the Rockies, Sierras, and Cascades, you'll also find glaciers. Once you've arrived at your glacier, walk out on it if you can. Feel its awesome power as you climb over its terminal moraine. Experience the beauty and sweep of its seemingly limitless curves that shape mountains and canyons. While you are standing on the glacier, imagine what the world was like two million years ago when most of North America and Europe were covered by sheets of ice just like the one you are now experiencing.

Little Misqually Glacier is one of several relatively small glaciers permanently affixed to the flanks of Mount Rainer in Washington.

A vast sea of ice, Johns Hopkins Glacier, winds its way like a great snowy highway through the mountains of Glacier Bay National Park in Alaska.

OPPOSITE
The sparkling waterfalls on Lunch Creek in Glacier National Park, Montana, leap and glide into the valley because a glacier lowered the riverbed, leaving the creek's tributaries high above the new floor.

GLACIER NATIONAL PARK

Straddling the Continental Divide in Montana, Glacier National Park contains some of the most beautiful primitive wilderness in the United States. In addition to glaciers, the park offers a wealth of rugged mountains, gorgeous alpine valleys, rivers, streams, and more than two hundred glacier-fed lakes.

The glaciers in the park are not as large as our planet's greatest glaciers, some of which are found in national parks in Alaska, but they are enchantingly beautiful. Grinnel Glacier, the park's largest, is about one and a half miles long and about one mile wide. Nearly five hundred feet thick, it lies on the northern flank of Mount Gould above Many Glacier Valley. Along with its glaciers, the park is renowned for its inspiring mountains, many of which resemble the jagged red peaks of the Canadian Rockies farther north.

Established in 1910, the park was once part of the Blackfeet Indian Reservation. Along with the Waterton Lakes National Park just across the border in Canada, Glacier National Park forms Waterton-Glacier International Peace Park, which was created by the two governments in 1932. The park is remarkable for its wealth of wildlife: Rocky Mountain goat and sheep, bear, moose, elk, deer, coyote, wolf, and lynx. An abundant supply of fish, especially cutthroat trout, fills its streams and lakes.

The park is a geological wonderland. If you visit Glacier, be sure to take in the Lewis Overthrust, a remarkable ridge high in the mountains that is made of colorful layers of rock much like those you see in the Grand Canyon. The ridge was formed when the earth split apart and one section was thrust up and over the other.

*This kettle pond near Nahma, Michigan, looks more
like a backyard swimming pool than a natural lake.
But like many of the world's lakes, it was created by
a glacier during the Pleistocene Era.*

*PRECEDING PAGES
The slow journey of a glacier comes to an end at
the sea, the point where icebergs calve from
ice caps as the action of waves causes large
chunks of ice to break off.*

CHAPTER THREE

*These huge boulders were left behind when glaciers
moved through what is now Yosemite National Park
in California. Glaciers have great power to form
the terrain over which they flow.*

CHAPTER THREE

Moving with slow and steady determination,
Romanche Glacier flows down to the sea in the
Beagle Channel of Chile, where its pace quickens
suddenly into fast flowing waterfalls.

*Where Mendenhall Glacier comes down to the
sea near Juneau, Alaska, the blue-green ocean
pales next to the intense blue of the glacier's
densely packed ice.*

CHAPTER THREE

FLOATING SPLENDOR

During the night of April 14, 1912, on her maiden voyage across the North Atlantic, from Southhampton, England, to New York, the Titanic collided with an iceberg and sank. The state-of-the-art ocean liner was the largest ship then afloat. About fifteen hundred people died in the frigid water when the great, unsinkable ship went down in what was one of the greatest sea disasters in history, celebrated ever since in song and legend.

For many of us, learning about the Titanic's sad fate was our first introduction to icebergs: enormous masses of ice that float across the sea and give navigators nightmares. Most of us have never seen an iceberg, much less set foot on one. But we all know the iceberg's notorious reputation as a destroyer of ships and its more friendly character as a home for wayward penguins.

The frigid loveliness of these great floating disasters waiting to happen has been reported by explorers and seafarers for centuries. They have described the icebergs' great beauty and color, comparing them to enormous whales, gothic cathedrals, mountains, pyramids, and palaces. Observers all note their startling whiteness, which scientists tell us is caused by tiny, closely spaced gas cavities throughout the ice and the tiny waterfalls and rivulets of water that flow down gullies and cracks in their sides. An iceberg is likely to weigh more than an estimated (nobody has actually put one on the scales) million tons. Some are miles and miles long and tower more than forty stories above the ocean. As we all know this is not the whole picture because only one-eighth to one-tenth of an iceberg's total mass floats above the water.

North Atlantic icebergs, such as the one that sank the Titanic, come from the island of Greenland, which is almost entirely covered by a vast ice sheet a mile thick and more than seven hundred thousand square miles in size. Enormous tongues of ice extend from the edge of this vast ice field toward the sea. As the end of the glacier inches its way into the water, cracks in the ice along with the rough action of the sea cause massive chunks of ice to break away, or calve. The birth of an iceberg is usually accompanied by fierce cracking noises that sound like rolling thunder. Once it has broken loose from its mother glacier, a North Atlantic iceberg usually drifts across Baffin Bay and Davis Strait to the coast of Labrador. Only a few icebergs are carried by wind and sea currents into the Atlantic.

This antarctic giant in Admiralty Bay, King George, is made of ice that is at least five thousand years old. Some scientists believe glacial ice may be hundreds of thousands of years old.

CHAPTER FOUR

Ever since the Titanic went down, an international ice patrol has kept track of icebergs in the North Atlantic shipping lanes. The expense of maintaining the patrol is shared by 16 seagoing nations. Today, the patrol, which is run by the U.S. Coast Guard, uses reports from planes, ships, and satellites to record the position of icebergs and estimate their most likely course. Since most icebergs make their way into shipping channels during the spring, ships usually take a more southerly course during this season.

The farther south icebergs float, the more they break into smaller sections. House-size chunks that seafarers call bergy bits are nearly as dangerous to ships as full-sized bergs. Smaller, truck-size sections are called growlers for the sound they make as they slap through the waves. Navigators charting a course more than four hundred miles south of Newfoundland can relax their vigil somewhat. At that point virtually all icebergs, bergy bits, and growlers have gone the way of a snowball in July. Icebergs from Antarctica, their other major source, pose less danger to navigation because fewer ships ply southern waters, owing in part to the Panama Canal.

Whether they come from Greenland or Antarctica, icebergs have always been impossible for people to control. The U.S. Coast Guard has tried to destroy them with explosives, but this proved too expensive to pursue. Because an iceberg's submerged sections can tear open the hull of a ship, it is tricky and dangerous even to approach them. This makes it nearly impossible to haul them away from ocean shipping channels and explains why a scheme to drag icebergs to Saudi Arabia to supply fresh water was abandoned during the 1970s.

Wind not only propels icebergs through the water, it also erodes and shapes them. This ice arch is a short-lived version of the same kind of natural sculpting that created the rock formations in Arches National Park in Utah.

CHAPTER FOUR

This Greenland iceberg, floating off Labrador, will
spend only two years in the rough sea this far south.
If it had been larger, it might have stalked the seas
for as long as ten years.

A white fortress of ice drifts to sea from Antarctica,
a continent larger than Europe or Australia that
contains more than two-thirds of the world's fresh
water in the form of ice.

CHAPTER FOUR

CHAPTER FOUR

*A floating island of ice from Antarctica follows the
ocean current. It is not uncommon for icebergs
in the Southern ocean to measure more than
a hundred miles in length.*

OPPOSITE
*This icy behemoth, a grand antarctic iceberg,
is many times larger than the biggest North Atlantic
icebergs that are rarely more than a mile
or two across.*

ANTARCTIC ICEBERGS

The biggest iceberg ever reported was seen in the
waters off the coast of Antarctica, Earth's fifth largest
continent that sprawls across the region of the South
Pole. This enormous mass of floating ice was two hundred miles in length and sixty miles wide, making it
more than twice the size of the State of Delaware. By
comparison the largest iceberg ever measured in the
North Atlantic was only four miles long.

What causes this enormous disparity? One answer
is the immense size of the antarctic ice cap. It is about
five million square miles, which is an area larger than
the United States, Mexico, and Central America combined, and more than seven times as large as the
Greenland ice cap. This stupendous and lovely ice field,
the largest body of fresh water on earth, averages
about 7,100 feet thick. The ice cap increases the continent's surface area and makes Antarctica the highest
continent in terms of average elevation above sea level.

The frigid temperatures of Antarctica also account
for the enormous icebergs floating through the
Southern ocean. Antarctica is the coldest place on
Earth with the thermometer rarely climbing above
freezing (32 degrees Fahrenheit and 0 degrees centigrade). The coldest temperature ever recorded on the
planet was -128 Fahrenheit (-89 centigrade) at Vostok
Station in 1983.

Curiously, the animal most successful in adapting
to Antarctica's harsh environment is the human being.
Although fish, krill, penguins, seals, and whales thrive
in the offshore waters, only a few insects and tough
plants can survive in the harsh interior. In 1911
Norwegian explorer Roald Amundsen was the first
human—and possibly first creature of any kind—to
reach the South Pole. Today, scientists from a dozen
countries maintain year-round research stations on the
continent.

CHAPTER FOUR

*Glowing in the eerie light of the long arctic sunset,
icebergs are calved from one of Alaska's many
glaciers as its leading edge glides slowly into the sea.*

CHAPTER FOUR

*Alone and forlorn, this bergy bit in Prince Christian
Sound, Greenland, is unlikely ever to be carried out
to sea and will probably melt away near shore.*

*FOLLOWING PAGES
Like dollops of cream on pudding, small icebergs
from nearby glaciers fight for space on the surface
on Alaska's Portage Lake.*

CHAPTER FOUR

*These little growlers are about to melt away in an
Alaskan bay, but they'll leave behind pebbles,
boulders, soil, and even plant and animal life
collected long ago by their mother glacier.*

*Looking like huge melting scoops of vanilla ice
cream set adrift in a gigantic punch bowl, this
antarctic iceberg is pushed north by the prevailing
wind toward warmer seas.*

CHAPTER FOUR

THE FLOW OF LIFE

The Colorado River gets its start high in the Rocky Mountains where drops of water from melting snow form into tiny rivulets. They flow together into streams that race down the mountains to the valleys below the peaks that gave them birth. There the streams become a great torrent of rushing water. Nourished by tributaries from the Wind River Range in Wyoming and the Wasatch and Uinta Ranges in Utah, the Colorado River picks up power as it turns south toward Arizona and California, cutting canyons through desert plateaus in its rush to the sea.

Few of the world's rivers pass through more spectacular terrain than the Colorado, which passes through mountains, deserts, mesas, and the greatest slice in the crust of our planet's surface, the Grand Canyon. Few rivers have greater mystique, but despite the beauty and romance of this river's basin, the Colorado is not one of America's giant rivers. Its erratic, unreliable, and meager yearly flow is about the same as the Delaware River on the East Coast. By comparison, the mighty Columbia in the Pacific Northwest carries well over ten times this volume of water.

The Colorado has been called the Nile of America, and there are similarities between the two rivers. Both pass through arid terrain; both deposit natural silt in their fertile deltas, and most importantly, both rivers bring life and civilization to a vast desert basin. But after that the analogy fails. The Nile drains a basin of over one million square miles while the Colorado's basin is 245,000 square miles. The Nile is the world's longest river (4,160 miles from its source in Burundi to the Mediterranean Sea) while the Colorado travels just over a third that distance. Although the Nile passes through some of Africa's most spectacular scenery, it drops only 6,600 feet from Lake Victoria to the sea. The Colorado falls nearly three miles from the summits of the Rockies' tallest peaks, where it is fed by rich blankets of melting snow, to the Gulf of California.

The steepness of its course and rapidity of its descent from mountaintop to mountain valley, basin, canyon, and desert has made the Colorado one of the most romantic and dramatic rivers in the world. It traverses some of our planet's most spectacular scenery, much of which it is responsible for having created.

Working patiently for millions of years, the
Colorado River has created and continues to create
some of the most spectacular scenery on earth,
including this stretch of the Grand Canyon.

CHAPTER FIVE

There's a Hopi saying that perfectly sums up the relationship between human life and the world's rivers: "The blood of the land is the river of the body." The first civilizations appeared by necessity, not by design, along rivers—the Tigris and Euphrates in Asia and the Nile in Africa. Europe's second longest river after the Volga, the fabled Danube, has more than three hundred tributaries and nourishes an immense area of Eastern Europe. On its 1,770-mile journey from the Black Forest in Germany to the Black Sea, the Danube passes through or forms the borders of seven countries. It once was the northern border of the Roman Empire against a barbarian world.

The immense Yangtze is immeasurably important to China. From its source high in the Qinghai-Tibet Plateau, the river journeys east and south through mountains, great gorges, and plains for 3,900 miles. The Yangtze cuts China in two, spans nine provinces, drains an area of 695,000 square miles, and affects the lives of one out of every fourteen people on Earth. But most important is the Yangtze's role as China's great highway, accounting for up to eighty percent of the country's inland shipping.

India's most important river, the Ganges, supplies spiritual and agricultural sustenance to one of the world's greatest concentrations of people. The river is also sacred to Hindus as the mother river of earth. Flowing 1,565 miles from an ice cave in the Himalayas to the Bay of Bengal, the Ganges provides water for extensive crop irrigation in its upper section and has created a fertile plain downstream.

None of these great rivers is the world's mightiest. Second only to the Nile in length but carrying more water than the Nile, Yangtze, and Mississippi combined, the Amazon does not flow through one of the earth's highly populated regions. The Amazon does not serve civilization; it has another task, one that many people say is more meaningful. On its 3,900-mile trip from the Andes Mountains in Peru through Brazil to the Atlantic Ocean, the mighty Amazon nourishes our planet's greatest rain forest. This wet, wild, green area of more than two million square miles teems with plants and animals, and it is vital to maintaining the health of the planet.

Like all rivers, the Amazon plays a basic role in the hydrologic cycle: the circulation of water from the oceans to the atmosphere through evaporation and back to the land as fresh water through precipitation and then back to the ocean. Without rivers—the lifelines of the ecosystems through which they flow—life on earth would not be as we know it.

*The earth's mightiest river, the Amazon, drains the
world's largest basin, more than two million square
miles, and nourishes the world's greatest rain forest.*

CHAPTER FIVE

Often mistaken for a stagnant swamp, the Florida Everglades is a wide, shallow, slow-moving river, fed by water from Okeechobee Lake and Big Cypress Swamp.

OPPOSITE
Dwarf cypress trees put down deep roots in the marshy lowlands kept wet by the Florida Everglades, a subtropical land of dense heat and thick swarms of insects.

A RIVER LIKE NO OTHER

Let's get one thing straight right away. The Everglades is not a swamp but a river. The Everglades is surrounded by swampland and look like a swamp with still water, saw grass, hammocks (islandlike masses of vegetation), mangrove forests, and a lot of black muck. But all is not as it seems in the Everglades.

The definition of a river is a large body of water that flows over land in a long channel. Most rivers begin high in mountains and are fed by melting snow, glaciers, or springs. But a river also can be fed by an overflowing lake. The Everglades is fed by water from Lake Okeechobee and Big Cypress Swamp in southern Florida. The swampy river is about five thousand square miles in size and flows slowly toward the sea in a broad channel. Limestone rims the area, acting as a natural retaining wall between the nearby ocean and the Everglades, with a highest point of only seven feet above sea level.

The Everglades pulses with life, including several endangered species, such as the crocodile, alligator, egret, bald eagle, and Florida panther. The greatest danger to these species is another species—human beings. Beginning in the late-nineteenth century, large tracts of the Everglades were drained because it was believed that the area was potentially rich for agriculture.

Only land directly adjacent to Lake Okeechobee was ever farmed, because in 1939 great fires spread across the Everglades as the result of overdraining. Despite this warning, immense retaining walls were constructed along the south shore of Lake Okeechobee during the 1960s, and large parcels of land were developed in Big Cypress Swamp, disrupting the natural flow of water into the Everglades and further threatening plant and animal life.

CHAPTER FIVE

81

*Thailand's Wat River flows through dense tropical
forests in the northern part of the country. For
centuries elephants have hauled teak that was
cut in the forest to the river so the logs could
be floated to market.*

CHAPTER FIVE

*In this area near Aswam, Egypt, the Nile begins
to broaden until it eventually becomes almost twelve
miles wide, bathing a wide swath of desert with
life-giving water and silt.*

CHAPTER FIVE

It is easy to see how Alaska's Delta River got its name. Like the delta of the Nile River in Africa, this river's delta forms the triangular shape of the Greek letter delta.

LIFE ON THE DELTA

New Orleans, one of America's most romantic and exotic cities, would not exist were it not for the Mississippi River. Or at least it would not be located where it is. Without the Mississippi and the vast delta it has created, the site of New Orleans would lie beneath the water of the Gulf of Mexico.

Like many of the world's great rivers—the Nile, Niger, Rhone, Volga, Brahmaputra, and Ganges—the Mississippi drops millions of tons of dirt and rock at its mouth where it flows into the sea. As a river moves through the land, it carries with it the products of erosion and rock decay from along its entire length. The Mississippi Delta receives silt from a riverbed that is about 3,750 miles long, which is the combined length of the Mississippi, the major river of the United States, and its major tributary, the Missouri River.

Deltas build up because the flow of water in virtually every river slows down dramatically at its mouth, especially when the river flows from a steep slope to a flatter one. The material that is dissolved in the water and is usually invisible mixes with lake or ocean water and settles to the bottom. Over time the material builds up and a delta is formed. Deltas rarely form when the coastal plain drops off steeply into the sea or where ocean or tidal currents carry sediment away.

Geologists believe that the creation of the Mississippi's current delta began about 1500 B.C. They also speculate that there may have been as many as three earlier deltas before this one. Like other deltas —the word comes from the Greek letter *delta*, which has the same triangular shape as the Nile Delta—the Mississippi Delta is immensely fertile. It is an area of swamps and bayous, inhabited by wildlife and human beings who alone have tried to control and regulate the ongoing delta process with the construction of countless dams and levees.

As the broad and slow-moving Mississippi River flows past Hannibal, Missouri, its lazy rhythm stirs memories of Huckleberry Finn and Tom Sawyer.

CHAPTER FIVE

*Mountain born and bred, the Colorado River begins
high in the Rockies of its namesake state, then it
drops nearly three miles following a 1,400-mile
course to the Gulf of California.*

*The Columbia River cuts through the Cascades and
the Coastal Range creating gorges great and small,
including tiny but extremely beautiful Onconta
Gorge in Oregon.*

CHAPTER FIVE

FALLING WATER

Nothing quite prepares a traveler for his or her first view of the Lauterbrunnen Valley in central Switzerland. This U-shaped gorge has vertical walls towering fifteen hundred feet. The valley is surrounded by the snowy summits of the Jungfrau, Eiger, and other peaks of the Bernese Alps. The Lauterbrunnen is a nearly unbelievable work of nature not only because of its stunning topography but also because water falls in glorious cascades from the cliffs to the valley floor.

The "tail of the pale horse ridden by Death in the Apocalypse" is the way the poet George Gordon, Lord Byron, described Staubbach Waterfall, which plunges nearly one thousand feet before dissolving almost entirely into fine spray. Trummelbach Falls has sliced a 1,283-foot path through deep cuts in the side of the cliff. The power of the Trummelbach, the highest waterfall in Switzerland, is almost hypnotic as tons of cascading white water plummet through winding fissures, leaping and boiling in a series of great eroded potholes.

Waterfalls seem to have a power over us that is unique in nature. They delight us, captivate us, intrigue us, and mystify us. Where does all that water come from? Where will it go? How can so much water keep falling and not run dry? The answer to these questions lies in the fact that a waterfall is just a vertical section of a river. This definition doesn't explain the unceasing fascination waterfalls hold for most people, but it helps us understand what a waterfall is.

A waterfall occurs anywhere there is an abrupt drop in a river that causes the flow of water to become vertical. A waterfall will run dry no sooner than the river of which it is a part. Generally speaking, a waterfall of relatively low height and less steepness is called a cascade, as is a series of small waterfalls along a stretch of river. Less dramatic sections of turbulent water that may contain a fall or two are termed rapids.

Compared to many other geological features, waterfalls are very short-lived. Over time rivers tend to smooth out irregularities, such as waterfalls, cascades, and rapids, that impede their flow. The patient river accomplishes this time-consuming task by the joint process of erosion and deposition until it has made its channel as

One of earth's most beautiful valleys,
Lauterbrunnen in central Switzerland is famous for
its sparkling springs and towering waterfalls, such
as Staubbach that falls nearly a thousand feet.

CHAPTER SIX

slick and smooth as a newly paved city street. Geologists study waterfalls and the terrain around them partly because of this impermanence and partly because so many of them came into existence such a short time ago. Some waterfalls are just a few thousand years old.

The greatest concentrations of high dramatic waterfalls occur along the edges of the great plateaus and escarpments in Africa and South America. Angel Falls on the Rio Caroni in Venezuela plunges 3,212 feet from the Auyan-Tepui Mesa; it is the highest and arguably the most spectacular falls on earth. The African and South American plateau falls are the oldest on our planet and came into existence during the last part of the Tertiary Period, a time of great geological uplifting. As plateaus and scarps rose up above their surroundings, immense waterfalls, such as Angel Falls, appeared where rivers crossed the boundary between plateau and lowland.

Some of Africa's highest falls, including Kalambo Falls (1,401 feet tall) located near Lake Tanganyika, and Tugela Falls (3,110 feet tall) in South Africa, were created during this same period under similar geological conditions. The most famous waterfall in Africa is not among the highest. In 1855 British explorer David Livingston was trekking through south-central Africa. Along the Zambezi River, he came upon one of Earth's most stupendous sights: a gigantic waterfall about 420 feet high. The roar of the falls was so great that Livingston had heard it more than 25 miles away. He named the waterfall Victoria Falls in honor of his queen and pronounced his discovery the greatest falls on earth. Today, geologists have determined that Victoria Falls was formed as the river carved a steep and narrow chasm along a fracture zone in the earth's crust.

Not everyone agrees with Dr. Livingston that Victoria is the greatest waterfall on earth. You be the judge. Should height, volume of water, beauty, or some combination of the three be the criterion? Curiously, the highest falls—especially those over a thousand feet—almost never issue huge volumes of water compared with shorter ones, such as the Khone Falls on the Mekong River in Laos. Although it is only 45 feet tall, the mighty Khone discharges twice as much water as Niagara Falls, the second greatest waterfall in terms of volume.

*Mist from a spring-fed waterfall on Clark's Creek at
Lost Canyon on the Buffalo National River,
Arizona, allows moss and ferns to grow along the
riverbed in this otherwise arid region.*

CHAPTER SIX

*When the Blue Nile runs rich with water during the
rainy season, Nisisat Falls is a billowing storm
of swiftly falling water*

CHAPTER SIX

*The constant wearing action of the gentle cascades
of this waterfall in an Oregon forest will eventually
erode the falls and flatten the riverbed.*

CHAPTER SIX

The world's tallest waterfalls are at the edges of high plateaus. When Victoria Falls is viewed from above, the abruptness with which the plateau drops away is dramatically evident.

OPPOSITE
Even a small waterfall, such as Laurel Falls in Great Smokey Mountain National Park, Tennessee, provides a spot for blissful repose and contemplation.

WATERFALL CLASSIFICATION

Geologists are able to predict accurately where waterfalls are likely to occur. They know that waterfalls are only rarely found on a desert or plain, but are likely to appear in regions of mountains or plateaus. In fact, one way geologists classify waterfalls is simply to identify the kind of region in which they occur.

The highest waterfalls, such as Angel Falls in Venezuela or Tugela Falls in South Africa, almost always occur at the edges of high plateaus. Victoria Falls, although not as high as these others, is also classified as a plateau waterfall.

Another major kind of waterfall occurs along a fall line, the point where a range of mountains drops steeply to a coastal plain. Many major East Coast cities, including Trenton, Philadelphia, Baltimore, and Washington, were built on the fall lines of rivers above which navigation was difficult or impossible. The most spectacular fall-line waterfalls are not in the United States. These include Churchill Falls in Labrador, Jog Falls near Karnataka, India, and the stupendous Paulo Afonso Falls on the Sao Francisco River in Brazil, which at one time or another has been proclaimed the world's greatest.

The highest waterfall in the United States, 2,425-foot Yosemite Falls in California, is typical of the third major category: waterfalls that occur in mountains or other regions once covered by glaciers. This kind of waterfall also appears, as you would expect, in the Alps, Sierra Nevada, Rockies, and mountains of New Zealand's South Island along with mountainous areas of Iceland and the fjord region of Norway.

*Victoria Falls on the Zambezi River seems to
disappear in the mist as it makes its four-hundred-
foot drop but the thunderous roar of the falls can be
heard from as much as 25 miles away.*

CHAPTER SIX

The highest and most dramatic waterfall on earth,
Angel Falls on the Rio Caroni in Venezuela,
plunges more than three thousand feet from the
Auyan-Tepui Mesa.

CHAPTER SIX

The power of erosion at Niagara Falls is so dramatic, you can almost watch it happen. Geological measurements indicate that the waterfalls retreat upriver about three feet every year.

HONEYMOON FALLS

Cities are often built near waterfalls because they can be used to generate hydroelectric power, one of the cheapest and most environmentally sound energy sources. Power generated by the Falls of Saint Anthony on the Mississippi drove the great flour mills that helped turn Minneapolis into a major city. Farther east the first textile mills in New England were built along the line where rivers from the Appalachian Mountains descend abruptly to the coastal plain, creating many waterfalls.

The grandest of these falls is one of the most famous spectacles in the United States: Niagara Falls on the Niagara River that separates Buffalo, New York, from Ontario, Canada. A stunning wall of water that sounds like thunder even miles away, the falls drew so many honeymooning couples in the 1930s and 1940s that "going to Niagara Falls" became a euphemism for getting married. Horseshoe Falls on the Canadian side of the river is one-half mile wide and 160 feet tall, which is relatively short for a waterfall. But the volume of water plunging over the falls (195,000 cubic feet per second) makes Niagara a sight never to be forgotten.

Equally as impressive as its beauty is the staggering power of erosion at Niagara Falls. Geologists have taken measurements there since the mid-nineteenth century, and their figures show that Horseshoe Falls retreats about three feet in a year. At this rate the waterfall has moved about seven and a half miles upriver in the twelve thousand years it has existed.

*Horseshoe Falls on the Canadian side of the
Niagara River is as mighty as it is romantic.
One-half mile wide and 160 feet tall, the waterfall
discharges a phenomenal 195,000 cubic feet
of water every second.*

CHAPTER SIX

*One of the loveliest falls in the United States,
Bridalveil Falls, plummets off a dramatic
escarpment in Yosemite National Park in California.*

CHAPTER SIX

After a rain shower, this waterfall on Hilo,
Hawaii's Big Island, quickly swells from a trickle
to become a broad ribbon of surging water.

CHAPTER SIX

101

*Tumbling swiftly down out of the mountains, a
stream rushes into the Columbia River gorge over
Wahkeena Falls, adding the glimmer and thunder of
falling water to the dense green, quiet forest.*

*Autumn comes early to the Vermont mountains
brightening the trees with gold and yellow.
Even though it is late in the year,
underground springs keep Moss Glen Falls
brimming over with sparkling water.*

CHAPTER SIX

STILL WATER

Lake Geneva is surely the world's most civilized lake. It sweeps in a 43-mile-long crescent between the Jura Mountains and the Alps through a glorious valley in western Switzerland. On one end is the international and erudite city of Geneva; on the other is wealthy and sophisticated Montreux. Every mile of the lakeshore is fringed with vineyards, stunning chateaux, clinics for the rich and famous, and exquisite botanical gardens. Hovering in the distance is Mont Blanc, Europe's tallest mountain.

Lake Geneva itself helps to create this lovely environment. An ongoing exchange of heat between the water of the lake and the atmosphere produces an unusually mild climate for a mountainous region high above sea level. In a sense, the lake, which is more than one thousand feet deep, can be viewed as an immense thermal reservoir. Heat is stored for release when air temperatures drop, so that when it's bitter cold and snowing on Mont Blanc, you can stroll in shorts along the lake.

Like Lake Geneva, large lakes around the world have a great influence on the people who live near them. Lakes tend to stabilize an area's climate, making the land around a large lake useful for farming, recreation, wildlife, and industry. Warm winds blowing off a lake make it possible for certain kinds of crops to grow well when it would otherwise be too cold. The warming influence of Lake Ontario extends the growing season of southern Ontario into the autumn, making it possible to raise fruit and corn.

The fruit-growing belt along the eastern shore of Lake Michigan also depends on winds blowing off a lake. Cool winds in the spring delay the blossoming of fruit trees until the danger of frost has passed, while autumn winds hold off the frost until the fruit is ripe for harvest. Thousands of lakes in central Florida create a favorable climate for the delicate citrus crop there.

Lakes are ubiquitous, occurring virtually everywhere on earth. The Dead Sea on the Israel-Jordan border is a salt lake that is nearly four hundred square miles in size. It lies in one of the hottest, most arid regions in the world. The surface of the lake is 1,292 feet below sea level, the lowest point on earth. The biblical cities of Sodom and Gomorrah once sat on its shores, which are surrounded by steep, rocky cliffs. Too salty to support life, the Dead Sea is fed by water from the Jordan River.

One of the loveliest lakes in the world, Lake Geneva is surrounded by well-tended terraced vineyards, the magnificent Alps, and the picturesque cities of Geneva, Lausanne, and Montreux.

CHAPTER SEVEN

Utah's Great Salt Lake is nearly as salty and six times as large as the Dead Sea. It is a modern remnant of a far-larger prehistoric lake. Because of constant evaporation in arid climates, both salt lakes become saltier each year.

The world's largest lake, the Caspian Sea, spans an enormous area that is larger than the state of Colorado. Evaporation is lowering the Caspian's water level, a problem that threatens commercial fishing and navigation.

The biggest lakes are great, briny inland seas. But the best lakes—at least the ones most people probably think of when they think of lakes—are in the mountains where most of the world's lakes are found. Canada has nearly half of the world's lakes simply because more of the world's existing lakes were produced by glaciers than any other natural force. The great ice sheets that crawled over Canada, the northern part of the United States, and northern Europe between ten thousand and two and a half million years ago gouged out untold numbers of depressions in the bedrock, producing tens of thousands of rock-shored mountain lakes.

Glaciers also deposited rock debris and sediment that dammed up rivers and streams, causing still more lakes to form. As glacial ice retreated, it often left deep pits, called kettle holes, that became lakes when water filled them. Crater Lake in Oregon is another kind of mountain lake. It was created when the top of a volcano was blown off during a violent eruption. Unlike almost all other lakes, Crater Lake has no inlet or outlet; its water level is maintained by rain and snowfall. Lakes also form in places where the earth's surface has been warped or broken into immense down-dropped blocks that fill with water. Lakes Malawi (Nyasa) and Tanganyika in Africa's Great Rift valley were formed in this way.

Lakes are short-lived geological features. Almost as soon as one forms, streams begin to carry in sediment that starts filling it up. If the basin fills in so much that the lake begins to overflow, the outflowing stream erodes the lip of the basin and the lake drains. Biology also conspires against lakes, with organic material from vegetation causing shallow lakes to become bogs and ultimately dry land, which is the fate of all lakes.

Occupying a pit on top of a long-gone volcano,
Crater Lake in Oregon is one of the deepest lakes
in North America (1,931 feet). It is kept filled
entirely by rain and snow.

CHAPTER SEVEN

Reflecting the majesty of the Rocky Mountains, sparkling Moraine Lake in Canada's Banff National Park is part of our watery legacy from the last ice age.

CHAPTER SEVEN

*A pristine lake in the Fink River Gorge in
central Australia provides a welcome respite
from the vast desert that sprawls across the
earth's driest continent.*

CHAPTER SEVEN

109

Beautiful Isle Royale is the largest island in Lake Superior, but the island is strictly a summer pleasure, since ice and high waves make it almost inaccessible during the winter.

LAKE SUPERIOR

Carved out by the great Pleistocene ice sheets between ten thousand and to two and a half million years ago, the Great Lakes are the world's largest system of freshwater lakes. Lake Superior is the biggest, deepest, highest above sea level, and by many accounts, the loveliest of the five lakes. It also happens to be the largest body of freshwater in the United States.

The lake is 350 miles by 160 at its longest and widest and covers an area nearly as large as the state of Indiana. Lake Superior is so vast that it really is a great inland sea. Freighters and barges sail its waters during much of the year, carrying iron ore, taconite, lumber, wheat, copper, and other minerals to ports throughout the Great Lakes. The boats move out of Lake Superior through the locks of the Soo Canals at Sault Sainte Marie in northern Michigan that carry them around the rapids of the Saint Marys River into Lake Huron and points east.

Most of Superior's coastline is rocky and forested. Colorful sandstone formations called the Pictured Rocks rise along sections of the shore in Michigan. More than two hundred rivers empty into Lake Superior, many with waterfalls plunging over rocky headlands near the shoreline. This beauty accounts for the summer resorts, fishing villages, and state parks that line most of Lake Superior's accessible shoreline.

*The bold, rocky shoreline of Lake Superior,
the largest freshwater lake in the world, is more
pristine and less polluted than the shores of the
other Great Lakes.*

CHAPTER SEVEN

Grass Lake on the Pigeon River in Michigan is everything a lake should be. It is one of thousands of lakes in the northern United States and southern Canada that are the legacy of the last ice age.

*Fed by water melting from a nearby glacier,
crystal-clear Lake Saint Mary, like many of the
world's lakes, fills a basin cut by a glacier during
the last ice age.*

CHAPTER SEVEN

Plants growing in a lake at Great Meadows National Wildlife Refuge in Maine nourish insects, snails, and fish, which make a tasty dinner for the ducks and geese that pass through the reserve.

LIFE IN A LAKE

A lake creates a little world unto itself. In the upper waters, there is usually a good supply of light, heat, oxygen, and nutrients that are well distributed by currents and turbulence. This condition supports a wide range of life.

Water plants of all shapes and sizes live under the surface. Some are attached to the lake bottom, while others float free. This vegetation provides food for such water creatures as insects, snails, and fish, which in turn are eaten by waterfowl, such as ducks, geese, swans, flamingos, egrets, cranes, and cormorants. Larger land mammals, including moose, wolves, and cougars in North America and lions, tigers, and elephants in Africa and Asia, tend to congregate along lakeshores to drink water and feed.

At the bottom of the food chain are the life forms that are most abundant in virtually any lake: plankton, algae, and flagellates. In the lower levels of the lake water and in sediments on the bottom, the major life form is bacteria.

The balance of life in a lake is delicate. Toxic materials from industrial or domestic waste can seriously disrupt almost any lake's normal biological activity, usually by removing free oxygen from the water. Modern civilization also threatens this fragile balancing act by allowing agriculture pesticides and herbicides to be carried into lakes by streams and rivers, or by introducing sulfuric acid and other pollutants into the atmosphere that fall on lakes in the form of acid rain.

*This small lake in New Jersey will not be around
much longer. It has been gradually filling with silt
for the past forty years and is now well on its way
to becoming a marsh.*

CHAPTER SEVEN

*Badwater Lake in California is the lowest point in
the United States. Large deposits of salt and other
minerals rise above the lake's surface, looking
deceptively like ice flows.*

*Too salty to support life of any kind, the Dead Sea
on the border of Israel and Jordan in one of the
world's hottest, most arid regions is the
lowest point on earth.*

*Glimmering Moraine Lake in Banff National Park
is a large glacial lake that is named for the rocky
debris, or moraine, left behind by a glacier that
now forms the lake's shore.*

CHAPTER SEVEN

*A reminder of the far-distant past, this lava flow at
Shovel Point on the Little Palisades of Lake Superior
may have been revealed when the lake was carved
out of bedrock by gigantic ice sheets more than
ten thousand years ago.*

CHAPTER SEVEN

PARCHED EARTH

When you imagine a desert, you probably think of the Sahara, the world's greatest arid region—an awesome, naked land of shifting sand and timeless mazes of mesas, jutting spikes, wadis, and rock pillars. In its endless interior, steep scarps flatten into eroded country, and mountains of sand seem to be swallowing entire buttes and mesas, while the never-ending wind stirs up the constant dust.

The Sahara extends more than three thousand miles across North Africa from the Atlantic Ocean to the Red Sea, taking in most of six countries and large chunks of six more. The desert covers an area nearly as large as the continental United States. In Arabic *sahara* is the plural of desert, and in a sense, the Sahara is many deserts in one. As large as all the other deserts of the world combined, its range of features is stunning, from the eleven-thousand-foot black massif of Tibesti in northern Chad to the Qattara Depression in Egypt, a vast sinkhole of salt marsh and treacherous quicksand that drops more than four hundred feet below sea level.

The extreme dryness, or hyperaridity, of the Sahara is caused by the same dynamics of atmospheric circulation that have created all the world's deserts. The combination of incoming solar radiation and the planet's rotation drives this circulation of air. The Sahara's dryness actually begins in the humid tropics where the equator crosses Africa's midsection. There hot air rises, dumping rain as its cools and spreads toward the poles. Between 15 and 30 degrees north and south—the so-called horse latitudes—the air sinks and warms again. This prevents the formation of clouds and rain, and creates the parallel belts of parched earth that girdle the globe.

The subtropical high-pressure belt constantly renews the extreme dryness of the Sahara. Any moisture that happens to move south from the Mediterranean Sea is blocked by the Atlas Mountains of North Africa, adding to the harshness of the Sahara's climate. This vast high-pressure belt also dries out the earth's surface in the Arabian and Iranian deserts of the Middle East and the great Indian desert and the mighty Turkestan desert of central Asia. In eastern Asia almost nothing can live in parts of China's Takla Makan desert because any precipitation coming its way is waylaid by the Tibetan uplands. Somewhat less arid, the Gobi is eastern Asia's largest desert.

A rare oasis of palms fights for a minuscule supply of groundwater on the Sahara, the world's largest desert, that covers an area of North Africa larger than the United States.

CHAPTER EIGHT

The desert-making belt of high pressure extends across the Pacific where it has helped create the Chihuahua Desert in Mexico and the Sonora and Mojave deserts in the southwest part of the United States. It is also responsible for the semiarid conditions in the Great Basin between the Rockies and the Sierra Nevada.

South of the equator, the southern hemisphere's high-pressure belt has produced deserts that line South America's west coast and extend south into the Patagonia in the southern part of Argentina. One town in Chile's Atacama Desert, the world's driest area, has never recorded rain.

Across the Pacific, arid and semiarid deserts grip almost all of Australia, where soil has become impoverished and worn out with age. What little vegetation there is in the Australian Outback, which consists of four separate desert areas, has adapted to boom-and-bust cycles of drought interrupted by sudden, gully-washing rains. The dry, sandy Namib and Kalahari deserts, where the sand is so porous that rain is instantly absorbed and disappears, lie on the same latitudes in southern Africa. The only areas defined as deserts that are not subject to the dry vagaries of the horse latitudes are those of the Arctic and Antarctic, vast regions which have an average annual precipitation of less than about ten inches.

Once it was believed that deserts had simply existed as they are for all time. Today, geologists and other scientists realize that deserts change dramatically over time. During the past sixty-five million years, the Sahara's boundaries have advanced and retreated many times. Oak trees once grew in the Sahara highlands, and prehistoric rock paintings portray plentiful wildlife. But today, the Sahara and other deserts tend to be advancing rather than retreating. Desert areas account for about one-third of the earth's land areas. About one-sixth of the earth's population, nearly 750 million people, live in these dry, hot regions.

Although the twin high-pressure belts circling the planet created the deserts, people increasingly are helping and encouraging their advance across former frontiers. Marginal lands are cleared and plowed, trees are cut for fuel, livestock is allowed to overgraze, and irrigation sterilizes the earth with salt and alkaline residues. Each year the number of people who live in the desert increases, while the productivity of the land decreases. This process is not only occurring in third-world countries but also in the southwestern part of the United States. According to the United Nations, deserts claim some twenty-seven thousand square mile of new territory each year. This is an area slightly larger than the state of West Virginia. Since the time of our earliest civilizations, which were in the desert, people have fought against the desert. Could all of our labors one day turn to dust as people themselves speed the desert's relentless new advance?

The Namib Desert is a hot narrow strip of parched earth that lies along the Atlantic coast in southwestern Africa. It receives less than one-half inch of rain annually and is almost totally barren.

CHAPTER EIGHT

*One of the driest, most desolate places in the world,
San Pedro de Atacama in the desert of northern
Chile, gets almost no moisture because the Andes
block almost all the rain from the interior.*

*Salt and mineral deposits on Devil's Golf Course in
Death Valley, California, look deceptively like newly
fallen snow. But with temperatures often well above
100 degrees Fahrenheit, snow is unknown here.*

CHAPTER EIGHT

*Resembling the skulls of prehistoric beasts, rocks
bask in the eternal sun of the Australian Outback,
a semiarid desert that covers most
of earth's driest continent.*

*Mysterious Ayers Rock near Alice Springs,
Australia, rises suddenly from the flat empty plain
in the desert of north-central Australia.*

CHAPTER EIGHT

CHAPTER EIGHT

Desert plants are survivors. They have developed extensive root systems that serve both to hold them to the shifting sand and to allow them to draw nourishment from the largest possible area.

Struggling for survival, a lone yucca plant endures the blazing sun and seeks moisture on a field of dunes at White Sands National Monument in southern New Mexico.

DESERT ECOSYSTEMS

Deserts cover vast regions of every continent. But scientists do not yet have a full grasp of the ecology of deserts. To help them understand how life functions on deserts, biologists have identified several kinds of desert ecosystems. In the so-called cold desert of the Arctic and Antarctic, there is little precipitation and great temperature extremes. For most of the year, life is confined to a few shrubs and a very few trees. In spring and summer, life bursts forth briefly when many short-lived annual plants appear and migrating birds and animals return.

Another kind of desert in warmer, though not usually tropical, climates is typified by shrubs and thorn scrub. This kind of desert includes the Mojave and Chihuahua deserts in North America and the dry regions of interior Australia. A similar kind of region is known as the stem-succulent desert, which is confined mainly to the Sonora Desert of North America, the desert area between Peru and Argentina, and the Namib Desert in Africa. Cactus plants are found in these desert areas.

Herbaceous deserts, such as the Nullarbor Plain in the southern part of Australia, have few plants other than perennial herbs. Salt deserts often surround highly saline lakes, such as the Dead Sea or the Great Salt Lake. Very few organisms grow there. Sand-dune deserts, such as parts of the Sahara, are characterized by almost no moisture and very little life. In almost all arid regions, some water flows, creating wadis and watercourses. These areas often support trees or shrubs that have especially deep roots to tap water far underground. Specialized birds and animals feed on the vegetation of the watercourse desert.

*California's fascinating Mojave Desert is a semiarid
region that lies in the rain shadow of the Sierra
Nevada. This delicate area is increasingly threatened
by recreational and industrial development.*

*The temperature of the scorched sand in these dunes
in Death Valley, California, heats up to 165 degrees
Fahrenheit on a summer day.*

CHAPTER EIGHT

Precious rain falls only infrequently in the Namib Desert. Most of it is absorbed instantly, but enough water flows through the Kuiseb riverbed to leave behind a layer of cracked dry mud.

In the desert, water is a treasure more precious than gold. But on the broad flatlands of Great Sand Dunes National Monument, New Mexico, Medano Creek makes its presence known only briefly.

CHAPTER EIGHT

132

*The California Desert is on the move. It now covers
an area of 25,000 square miles. This is an awesome
place where scarce rainfall averages between
three and four inches a year.*

*Constantly shifting sand dunes, extremely high
temperatures, and almost no water make Death
Valley in south-central California one of the most
forbidding places in the United States.*

*The Pinnacles, a national park on the western coast
of Australia north of Perth, is filled with unusual
rock formations that are relics of persistent
erosion by wind and water.*

*Tree trunks fill a gully on Blue Mesa in the Petrified
National Forest in Arizona, where a mighty forest,
now frozen in time by the dry climate, once stood.*

*PRECEDING PAGES
Mighty sentinels of the desert, saguaro cacti that
grow in the Sonora Desert of southern Arizona are
coveted by people for home decor, and as a result,
the unusual plant is increasingly endangered.*

CHAPTER EIGHT

NATURAL SCULPTURE

Even a great river has intimate spots. On the Colorado River, these rare and wondrous places are found, surprisingly, where the river has cut a great slice into the earth's surface, the Grand Canyon. You will not find these secret spots from the canyon's rim but must hike deep inside the gorge.

Walk down into the canyon on Bright Angel Trail or Kaibab Trail from the south rim, or better still, choose North Kaibab Trail with its trailhead on the less developed north rim. On the way down, you drop through nearly two billion years of geology that has been revealed by the river below. At the bottom, with these ancient walls towering above you, walk along the sandy shore. If you can forget the thousands of feet that have trod there before you, imagine for a moment an earlier age when the river did its work alone—undammed and unspoiled—carving and cutting out the canyon.

For an even more intimate visit, climb aboard a dory or raft for a ride on the waters of the Colorado into the canyon. The rim with its cluster of civilization slowly disappears from mind as the river becomes a flowing stairway to the past, dropping twenty-two hundred feet over one hundred fifty rapids through an ever-deepening gash that exposes the earth's oldest geologic eras. Deep in the canyon, you can see the repeated geological processes of uplift, erosion, and deposit of rock and sediment. Multicolored rock, steep walls with deep bays, isolated towers, mesas, and figures that look like cathedrals or temples—depending on your own whim—display contrasting light and shadow as hues of stupendous beauty change constantly throughout the day. Plant life in surprising abundance varies from subtropical along the river to subarctic near the rim. Hundreds of ancient Indian dwellings dot the lower walls.

The great canyon of the Colorado, which used to be named the Grand River giving that name to the canyon, lies on the southern margin of the Colorado Plateau, one of the greatest concentrations of canyonlands in the world. These canyonlands are equalled only by the system of wadis, watercourses, mesas, and buttes that roll across the Sahara in North Africa and into the desolate and dry expanses of the Sinai Peninsula. Linked by the Colorado River and its tributaries, the breathtaking Colorado Plateau encompasses much of southern Utah and northern Arizona, along with the Four Corners area of New Mexico and Colorado.

*The layers of rock in the Grand Canyon show us
the way in which the surface of our planet has
been shaped by the constant interplay of the
powerful natural forces of uplift, erosion,
submergence, and decay.*

CHAPTER NINE

Geology, climate, biology, and human history combine to make the plateau unique. But it is particularly the uplifted layers of sedimentary rock, gouged over the millennia by rivers, streams, wind, and rain, that define the region, which contains more national parks than any other part of the United States. Between Arches National Park in eastern Utah, the site of more than two hundred natural stone bridges, and the spectacular Grand Canyon, three hundred miles to the southwest, lie four more national parks.

Canyonlands National Park is a maze of deep canyons and other features carved by wind and water. It includes a wealth of spires, pinnacles, and arches. Great mesas rise above the stunning landscape. The Colorado and Green rivers roar through Cataract Canyon, which contains one of the world's largest exposures of red sandstone. Island in the Sky, a plateau overlooking the junction of the Green and Colorado rivers, drops in giant steps more than two thousand feet to the canyon floor. Upheaval Dome, pushed upward eons ago probably because of the pressure of surrounding rock on underground salt deposits, has a crater one mile wide and fifteen hundred feet deep. Nearby are some of the finest Indian petroglyphs in North America, drawn a thousand years ago.

Southeast lies Capitol Reef National Park, named for its nearly unbelievable spine of striated rock, a geological history chart that rises from the Fremont River. Bryce Canyon is a vast red rock amphitheater cut into the side of a nine-thousand-foot plateau and filled with hundreds of rock formations with such names as Thor's Hammer and Gulliver's Castle. Zion Canyon, home of massive rock outcroppings, waterfalls, and hanging gardens, is a fifteen-mile long gorge one-half mile deep, cut by the Virgin River.

The Colorado Plateau is rich in vegetation and wildlife, including deer, bighorn sheep, and mountain lions. This was once the home of the Anasazi, the Indians who lived in the Southwest a thousand years ago. Today, Navajos live on a vast reservation sprawled across the southern part of the Colorado Plateau. Within the reservation lies Monument Valley, a stunning array of geological majesty, dramatic rock spires, and towers, some of which are more than a thousand feet tall and just a few yards in diameter. This is a wondrous place that lets us feel as though we are wandering from room to room in a great outdoor cathedral with rocks buttressing the walls and the sky for a roof.

Smooth as a fine-grained wood veneer, the stone of
Slickrock Canyon near Lake Powell in southern
Utah has been polished to a fine sheen over the
centuries by water working its quiet magic.

CHAPTER NINE

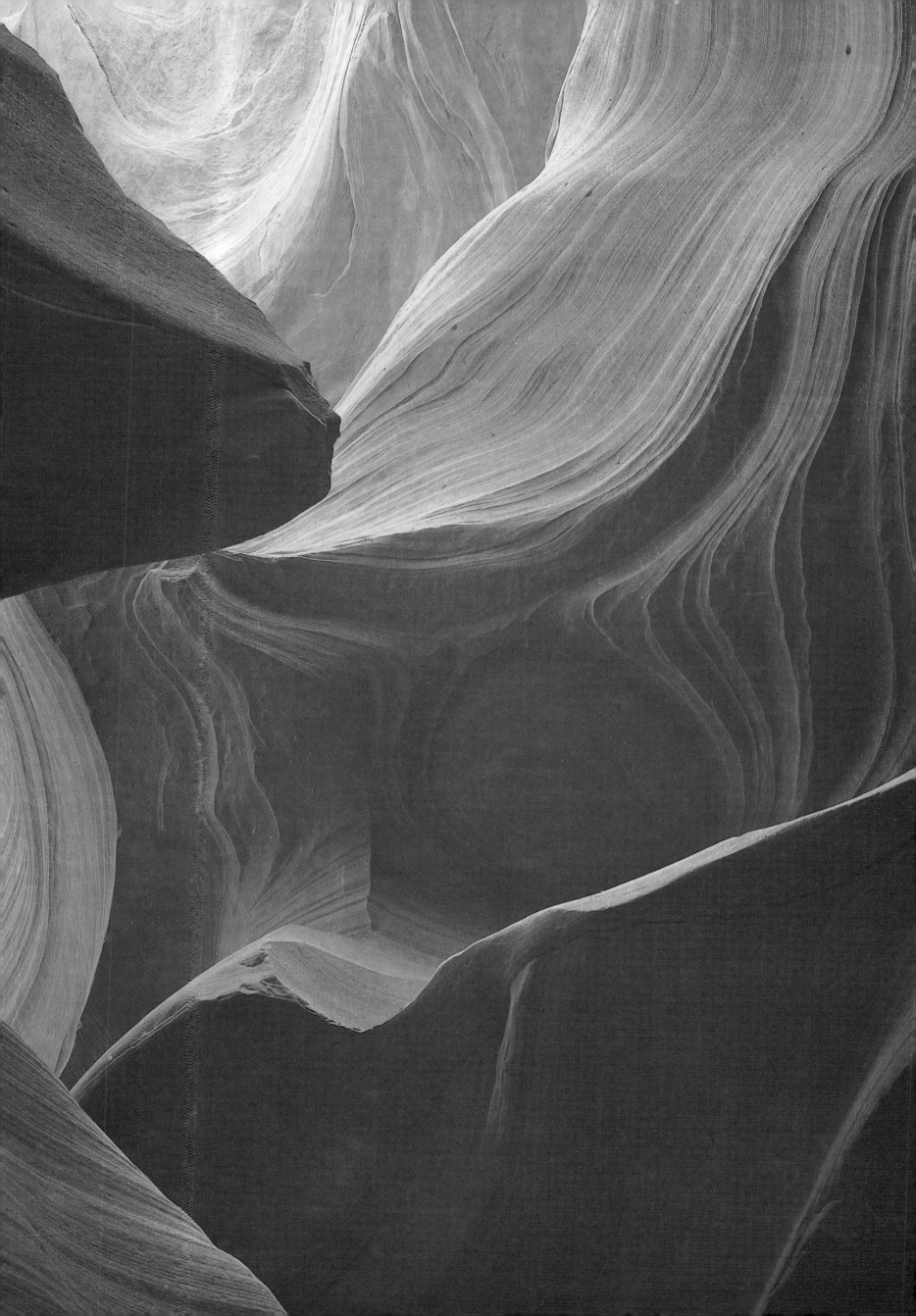

144

*Monument Valley at sunset is strikingly beautiful,
making an elemental statement about rock and sky
that awes us with its profound simplicity.*

*The natural sculpture gallery in Monument Valley
in the Navajo Reservation on the border
of Arizona and Utah contains one of the world's
most startling collections of rock formations, some
of which are a thousand feet tall.*

CHAPTER NINE

CHAPTER NINE

145

These unearthly rock formations, called hoodoos, were sculpted by wind and water in Bryce Canyon National Park, Utah. Erosion works swiftly here where canyon walls recede about one and a half feet each century.

BRYCE CANYON

The geology of Bryce Canyon is an open book, illustrated in fairy-tale colors. Castles and spires of stone tell a story of sixteen million years of epic battles between marauding water and wind and the rock of southern Utah. The scalloped edge of a high plateau, Bryce is actually not a canyon at all but a series of amphitheaters cut out of the Paunsaugunt Plateau.

On a grand scale, the geological formation containing Bryce Canyon resembles a loaf of bread that has been chewed away on one side. Erosion has taken about a dozen bites out of the pink cliffs that form the plateau's eastern edge. The Bryce escarpment, with its thousands of geological gargoyles and castellated spires, is what the relentless destructive powers of water and time have left behind. Under the onslaught of weather, nothing at Bryce remains the same for long, and the canyon is an excellent place to observe first-hand the forces that shape the surface of our planet.

A single summer cloudburst can carry off thousands of tons of gravel, sand, and silt to the Paria River and then on to the Colorado and into the Grand Canyon. As the ground thaws on warm days, you can hear the grinding, groaning, and grumbling of erosion at work. Water runs down crevices, rocks tumble, and gravel and pebbles shake loose from the sides of spires. The canyon's rim is receding one foot every 65 years. In geological terms, this is a fantastic rate of change.

OPPOSITE
Snow softens the harsh grandeur of Bryce Canyon National Park on a magical winter day when the air is crisp and clear, and the sun is bright.

The glorious architecture of nature is resplendent in Arches National Park, Utah, where two hundred natural arches rise gracefully from the Colorado Plateau. Here Turret Arch is framed by North Window Arch.

Utah's snowcapped La Sal Mountains are framed by Delicate Arch, one of many intriguing sandstone formations cut by wind and water in Arches National Park.

CHAPTER NINE

150

The highest point between the Rocky Mountains and the Alps, Harney Peak, rises 7,242 feet above sea level in the Black Hills of South Dakota. Erosion created these needles during the last seventy thousand years.

OPPOSITE
Lying below the tableland from which it has eroded during eons of infrequent but often torrential rain, the Badlands of South Dakota is a mystery land of eerie rock formations.

BADLANDS

Sometimes badlands are hard to find. This kind of land usually lies below the tableland from which it has eroded, so you can walk across rolling grasslands for miles without seeing any sign of badlands. Then suddenly you come upon a jumble of rock spires and buttresses, hundreds of feet high, lying just below your feet.

Badlands are found in semiarid country where rain is infrequent but often torrential, and wet weather can be followed by long periods of dry heat that bakes and firms the landforms molded by erosion. The Badlands in the southwestern part of South Dakota are earth's best and most extensive example of this kind of topography. Badlands are cut from deep alluvium and volcanic-ash deposits that were gouged and carved into stunning forms of all shapes and sizes by the action of wind and water. Beginning about thirty-five million years ago, rivers and streams running downhill from the Black Hills spread sand, mud, and gravel on the flatland to the east. For the first few million years, the floodplain built up faster than it could be eroded away. After that the balance changed, and the elements began attacking these deep layers of sediment.

The result is a tumult of spires, battlements, pinnacles, castles, and cathedrals almost a hundred miles long and fifty miles wide. The stark and angry landscape was feared and avoided by pioneers. But this unique wilderness is an unexpected region that contains a surprising wealth of natural beauty.

154

*Capitol Reef in Utah is a grand formation eroded
from sedimentary rock and sandstone that glimmers
in the clear sunlight with an inherent majesty no
government building can match.*

PRECEDING PAGES
*More than two billion years of steady erosion have
opened the surface of the earth at the Grand
Canyon to reveal a clear record of the geology of
our planet through eons of time.*

CHAPTER NINE

*Flowing along gently or raging through boulders
or narrow canyons, the Colorado River has slowly
cut into the earth's crust to a depth of about
one mile at the Grand Canyon.*

CHAPTER NINE

*The endless rugged beauty of the Grand Canyon
was a formidable obstacle to its earliest explorers.
One of them, Lieutenant Joseph Ives, pronounced
the area a "profitless locality."*

CHAPTER NINE

The Colorado River and its tributaries have carved
out thousands of canyons in southern Utah; many
of them are in Canyonlands National Park, a
fascinating maze of bluffs, mesas, and canyons
that seems to go on forever.

CHAPTER NINE

THE GREEN CANOPY

When you walk through the Rondonia jungle in western Brazil, a thick canopy of leaves fifteen stories above your head prevents the sunlight from reaching the ground. Travel by foot through the great forest does not require hacking your way through vines with a machete because there is little vegetation covering the ground. Walking is surprisingly easy; you might almost feel as though you are in a large well-tended arboretum. Where sunlight does get through the trees—along riverbanks or roadsides—a dense and tangled mass of bushes and vines grows up, giving credence to the popular image of a steamy and impenetrable jungle teeming with wildlife and uncontrollable vegetation.

The Rondonia is part of the Amazon River basin, a vast tropical rain forest (the modern term for a jungle). The largest rain forest in the world covers nearly thirty-five percent of South America, including most of Brazil and large parts of Bolivia, Peru, Ecuador, Colombia, and Venezuela. Like the other great rain forests in the Congo River basin in Africa and throughout much of Southeast Asia, Indonesia, and northern Australia, the Amazon forest lies on or near the equator where the climate is warm and wet all the year round. Temperatures generally average above 80 degrees Fahrenheit, and rainfall is more than ten feet each year.

The variety and profusion of trees in the Amazon rain forest is nothing short of phenomenal. Within a single square mile, there are more than a hundred species, none of which is dominant. The canopy, where the broad evergreen leaves of the great trees converge, is the heart of life in the rain forest. The upper canopy can be one hundred fifty feet or more above the ground, with a few enormous trees towering higher still. In places there are one or two mid-level canopies formed by palm trees and large tree ferns.

Climbing plants and hanging plants, which live entirely within the canopy with no connection to the ground, crowd the upper branches high above the forest floor. The forest canopy is also a territory inhabited by many rain forest animals. They are flying or climbing creatures, such as bats, tropical birds of dozens of varieties, hordes of insects, lizards, mice, monkeys, opossums, sloths, and jungle snakes. Some frogs and toads never come to earth during their entire lives. They even lay their eggs in water lying in little basins in the trees.

Intensely green tropical vegetation, which North Americans may recognize as familiar house plants, grows in thick profusion in this opulent rain forest.

A subvariety of the rain forest, the tropical seasonal forest is found in tropic and subtropic areas, such as Central America, southern Africa, India, eastern China, and Australia, that have definite wet and dry seasons. These forests have fewer species of trees and fewer climbing plants, and their canopy is not as high. But animal life in these forests is similar to that in the rain forest.

If you live in the eastern part of the United States, you have probably walked through one of Earth's most common kinds of woodland: the temperate deciduous forest. These great forests grow across the eastern section of North America and Western Europe as well as northwest China. They are filled with such trees as oak and elm that shed their leaves when the weather turns cold. Large animals, including bears, deer, and rarely now, wolves, live in these forests along with hundreds of species of smaller animals and birds.

The northwestern United States and the Rockies have few deciduous trees. The native forests consist of temperate evergreens, such as pine, fir, and spruce. Similar forests are found on the southern coast of Chile, the west coast of New Zealand, and the southeast coast of Australia. Since cool climates favor evergreen trees, temperate evergreen forests also appear on lower mountain slopes in Asia and Europe.

Boreal forests cover vast regions of northern Europe, Asia, and North America where winters are unusually harsh and the growing season is short. These extensive forests usually have a combination of two kinds of trees: spruce and fir or spruce and pine. Small mammals, beavers, mice, and porcupines live in the forest along with bears, caribou, foxes, moose, and wolves.

Forests first appeared in marshlands about 360 million years ago. These early forests were made up of enormous club mosses and ferns with trunks forty feet tall. After another hundred million years, these swamp forests were replaced by a profusion of seed ferns and primitive conifers. The first modern forests began appearing about two million years ago as the earth's climate became colder.

These early forests began taking on the look of today's forests after the last ice age about ten thousand years ago. At this same time, early people began clearing trees for agriculture. In the intervening ten millennia, human beings have had more influence on the world's forests than all natural factors combined.

In Logan Canyon in the Wasatch Mountains of northern Utah, sturdy pine trees take the higher, cooler rim while slender aspens prefer the warmer floor and sides of the canyon.

CHAPTER TEN

*Viewed from above, the green canopy of the
great rain forest in the Amazon River basin seems to
be impenetrable as it stretches out across two
million square miles of Brazil.*

CHAPTER TEN

*Mighty redwood trees, the largest ones still growing
in North America, create cool green shade in
Humboldt State Park in California.*

CHAPTER TEN

163

In this Costa Rican rain forest, many species of plants and animals live interdependent lives in a warm moist environment that extends from the forest floor to the canopy of treetops.

OPPOSITE
The luxuriant tropical rain forest in the Valle de Mai on Praslin Island in the Seychelles contains extraordinary plants that are found no place else on earth.

DESTRUCTION OF A RAIN FOREST

Forests, especially tropical rain forests, are disappearing at a frightening rate. Scientists estimate the toll is a staggering twenty-five thousand square miles lost annually. In Brazil's Rondonia rain forest, the rush of people into the area is so great that it brings to mind the land rush in the American West a century ago. In Rondonia settlers fleeing poverty-stricken lives elsewhere have been given large tracts of land by the federal government. Upon arriving in the rain forest, these newcomers immediately begin clearing their property by felling and burning trees until the land looks like a war zone. The damage to the environment has been severe since the mass movement to Rondonia began in the 1970s. It is estimated that as much as twenty percent of the rain forest there already has been destroyed. During the 1980s Rondonia's population doubled as the federal government completed paving a major road into the area.

The mass immigration has begun a dangerous process: First, farmers clear-cut the forest; then they harvest crops for a few seasons, using up the land's limited fertility. The farmers then leave the fields to cattle ranchers who graze their herds for a decade or two and finally abandon the exhausted land. Because rain forests grow so slowly, ecologists believe the forest may never be able to reclaim its lost territory.

CHAPTER TEN

Delicate birch trees grow throughout the northern hemisphere, but they are especially prevalent in the northeastern part of the United States, where they thrive in the thin rocky soil.

In this old-growth deciduous forest in the northern part of the United States, the sun has trouble peaking through the dense canopy of leaves high above the forest floor.

Raging out of control, a fire destroys a once-thriving evergreen forest near Libby, Montana. An estimated ninety percent of all forest fires in the United States are caused by people.

PRECEDING PAGES
This Pacific coast forest is an essential watershed. The thick layer of humus and soil on the forest floor, which is retained by the trees' long roots, prevents runoff even on steep slopes like this one.

CHAPTER TEN

*This deciduous forest, thick with solid, old trees,
in the Columbia Gorge of Oregon is unusual
in the West, where the typical forest is
made up of evergreens.*

CHAPTER TEN

*Even though some trees depend on the heat
of forest fires to release seed and others grow best
in the open sunlit spaces created by fires,
a fire-ravaged forest is a truly devastating sight.*

FIRE IN THE FOREST

Fires annually destroy about three million acres of forest in the United States. It is estimated that nearly ninety percent of these fires are caused by people. The rest are probably caused by lightning. At any given time during the summer, as many as a hundred forest fires can be roaring somewhere across the nation. Fortunately, most of these fires are small and less destructive than the great fires that destroyed hundreds of acres of Yellowstone National Park in 1988.

Fires in forests feed on fallen leaves, twigs, and other decaying material on the ground. To extinguish a fire, you usually have to contain or remove this highly flammable material. Fire crews typically attempt to slow a fire's progress by spraying the layer of fuel with water or fire-stopping chemicals. Then they dig a fire line (a wide strip of land from which all brush, logs, and trees have been removed) around the fire. Brave fire fighters known as smoke jumpers respond to the call of a fire lookout and parachute into otherwise inaccessible areas to dig fire lines.

Once a fire line has been cleared, fire fighters often ignite backfires between the fire line and the blazing forest fire to remove additional fuel and widen the fire line. In a process called prescribed burning, foresters occasionally set small fires on the floor of an unburned forest in order to eliminate fuel for a potential fire. This practice is highly controversial.

*Fire rushes along the forest floor, fed by fallen
leaves, twigs, and other decaying material on the
ground. The heat with which this highly flammable
material burns lifts the fire into the trees.*

CHAPTER TEN

This imposing bamboo forest near Narita, Japan, could be considered a grassland rather than a forest because bamboo is a kind of grass that grows a hundred feet tall in warm or tropical regions.

Many kinds of trees, bushes, and other plants prosper in this flourishing temperate hardwood forest, where a fairly mild climate with plenty of seasonal rain encourages lush growth.

SEAS OF GRASS

The Flint Hills roll north and south across eastern Kansas in a fifty-mile-wide swath. Scattered among the low hills and valleys lie miles and miles of rolling prairie. Dozens of kinds of green, red, and golden grasses, some as high as six feet tall, ripple in the wind. Great trees grow along streams. This is a country of cattle and cowboys, stone houses and barns. Because of a geological oddity, the region is the largest remaining tall grass prairie in the United States.

Prairie used to extend from Ohio to Kansas and from Texas to Canada, a sea of tall grass with hundreds of kinds of wildflowers covering more than four hundred thousand square miles. Today, except for the Flint Hills and a few small preserves scattered through the Midwest, the tall grass prairie is gone—victim to city, road, farm, and ranch. Cultivation, more than any other factor, destroys prairie, and over the course of a century, the great American tall grass prairie became the corn belt.

The Flint Hills prairie escaped destruction because its rocky topsoil is too thin and insubstantial for agriculture. The hills consist of limestone, embedded with flint, that was deposited by an inland sea two hundred million years ago. Prudent grazing has kept the prairie pristine, and the emerging sense that grassland is worth saving is likely to keep it that way. Each year brings more prairie preservation and prairie restoration activity, perhaps because people yearn for the past and for something that endures.

The remaining American tall grass prairie and the largely untouched short-grass prairie of the Great Plains are part of what was once Earth's greatest single ecosystem: grasslands. Before people began farming in earnest about ten thousand years ago, grasslands covered nearly half of the planet's total land surface. Prairies represent a major variety of grassland, one of the four major kinds of vegetation that cover the earth along with forests, desert shrub, and arctic or alpine tundra.

Large prairies girdle the globe, from the American Midwest to the great basins stretching from Hungary to Manchuria in China and along the coastal areas of Australia. Almost anywhere it is flat and humid, there is grassland. Argentina's vast Pampa, a prairie region nearly as large as America's Midwest, is an endless sea of tall grasses and wildflowers, punctuated here and there with trees along the banks of rivers and streams. The Pampa has retained more of its natural condition than its American counterpart because it has not been widely cultivated. Since Spanish colonial times, the region has been used primarily for grazing enormous herds of freely roaming cattle that are watched over by bands of gauchos, Argentine cowboys. Gradually now, as the demand for farm products mounts, the eastern Pampa is being cultivated, and the prairie along with the cattle and gauchos has retreated to the west.

*The grasses and sedges that dominate the Konza
Prairie of central Kansas maintain their ascendancy
by creating a dense ground cover that keeps other
kinds of plants from reaching full maturity.*

CHAPTER ELEVEN

Strictly speaking, the Great Plains of North America stretching from western Texas north through western Kansas, eastern Colorado, Nebraska, and the Dakotas into Canada are considered steppes not prairie. The difference is the kind of grass. These North American steppes, like the great steppes in central Asia and the veld in South Africa, grow shorter grass of fewer varieties and irregular distribution than prairie lands. These short grasses (spear grasses, feather grasses, and fescue) can adapt to drought conditions in dry climates better than the tall grasses of the prairie.

The vast grasslands of the African savanna teem with wildlife running free under endless open skies. Typically lying in subtropical areas that have a dry season in summer and a rainy winter, savannas also spread across Central America, Brazil, India, Southeast Asia, and Australia. They are often marginal areas, separating rain forests from deserts. Trees grow singly or in erratically spaced bunches, and the ground is covered with shrubs, herbs, and coarse grasses of many kinds.

Grasslands appeared on the earth's surface millions of years ago. Some developed on bare, dry land that had become overgrown with lichens and moss that was gradually replaced by herbs and grasses. Other grasslands evolved where watery areas filled with submerged plants drained, forcing the plants to adapt to dry conditions. Many early civilizations grew up in grassy areas of the world, and the process of turning grassland into farmland began early on in human history. The area surrounding the Mediterranean Sea has been occupied by human beings for so long that it is impossible to determine the original character of the land. But scientists believe that the deserts now found on the shores of the Mediterranean were once grasslands rich with life.

Indian paintbrush adds vibrant color to the
shortgrass and semidesert plants that grow on the
flatlands near Hayes Ridge in the Chisos Mountains
of Big Bend National Park in West Texas.

CHAPTER ELEVEN

Purple prairie grass is one of the few plants that can survive under the harsh conditions found in the dry, sandy grasslands near Berlin, Nevada.

GRASSLAND ECOSYSTEM

The grassland ecosystem is fragile and complex; it is balanced in a highly organized food web of producers, consumers, and decomposers. The destruction or removal of one species of plant or animal will often have a powerful effect on neighboring life forms by disrupting the balance.

The dominant plants, grasses and sedges, compete with herbaceous plants for ground space. They are usually successful because grasses create a dense cover that prevents other plants from reaching full maturity. These grasses are categorized according to their height. The longest grasses grow in tropical areas, and tall grasses with flowering stems are found in humid, temperate regions, such as the American Midwest. Shorter grasses are found in more arid steppe regions.

Grasslands used to be home to vast hordes of grazing animals along with several species of predators accompanying them. Immense herds of bison and pronghorn antelope once roamed the American prairies, preyed on by coyotes and bobcats. In Asia wild cattle, antelopes, wild horses, stags, and boars were pursued relentlessly by wolves and foxes. Several kinds of kangaroo inhabit the grasslands of Australia, with the dingo, a kind of wild dog, as their main predator.

Today, most of these grassland animals have been greatly reduced in number and all but eliminated as people use their former ranges to graze sheep, cattle, horses, and goats. In a few places, such as the managed game reserves in Africa, wild and domestic animals intermingle in the same grassland area. But for the most part, people look on these wild animals, along with their predators, as intruders.

*Hearty neneo shrubs dot the Patagonian upland
near Esquel in Chubet Province, Argentina. This
vast area is an inhospitable semiarid plateau where
shortgrass and shrubs struggle for survival.*

CHAPTER ELEVEN

On the Serengeti in Tanzania, Maisai herdsmen help along the grassland's natural cycle by setting fire to the dry grass each year as they have done for countless centuries.

PRAIRIE FIRES

When European settlers came to the great North American prairies, they found vast expanses of open land and rich soil well-suited to agriculture. But life on the open plains was not without danger. The settlers' diaries are filled with stories of devastating prairie fires. These wildfires burned with fierce heat and moved with incredible speed. One prairie fire reported in the 1880s moved so quickly that it overtook a man on horseback. There was nothing the farmers and ranchers could do to stop a fire; they just had to wait until it burned out or came to a river that was too large for the fire to leap.

Prairie fires usually occur in early spring or late fall. Most are started by lightning. It wasn't until the 1930s that people realized that this threat to human life on the prairie is essential for the life of the prairie itself. Prairies need fires to survive. Prairie plants have evolved in such a way that they actually benefit from seemingly devastating fires. Unlike forest plants that have much of their biomass (leaves and branches) high above ground level, prairie plants have most of their biomass (roots) underground. When a fire burns through a prairie, only debris and the tops of living plants are destroyed. This frees important nutrients to return to the soil.

After a fire burns a prairie, the ground is blackened. It absorbs and holds heat from the sun, extending the prairie's growing season by warming up the soil in spring or keeping it from freezing in the fall. Prairie fires also kill off plants that are not native to the prairie. This keeps the forest from encroaching on open land and encourages the growth of plants likely to thrive in this ecosystem.

*The awesome power of a prairie fire is frightening,
but unlike forests that can be totally decimated by
fire, prairies actually depend on fires to prosper.*

FOLLOWING PAGES
*Emerging from a thick blanket of snow, the
shortgrass prairie in Badlands National Park,
South Dakota, will soon come alive with green
shoots and bright wildflowers.*

CHAPTER ELEVEN

Like tiny triumphs of spring, wildflowers pop up on the grasslands in Serengeti National Park in Tanzania at the end of the winter rainy season.

THE SERENGETI

A land that time seems to have forgotten, the Serengeti is a vast ecological haven in eastern Africa. Much of this still largely undisturbed grassland is part of Serengeti National Park in Tanzania, a region that boasts the greatest concentration of large mammals in the world.

Waves of spear and wire grass roll across the Serengeti's broad plains, interrupted only by clumps of brush. Here and there grows a squat, strange-looking baobab. This short, stout tree has a trunk that is exceeded in size only by the sequoia. Protected from destructive human beings, the land looks much as it did thousands of years ago. Seemingly endless herds of migrating wildebeest roam free. Vast hordes of striped zebras dot the plain, along with gazelles, buffaloes, giraffes, and elands. The profusion of wildlife is stunning. Antelope, hartebeest, waterbuck, and impala also graze on the grassy fields. The Serengeti is home to the elephant, the world's largest land mammal, and the giraffe, the tallest mammal.

The herbivores of the Serengeti, whose eating habits have restricted the growth of trees, are accompanied by various omnivores, such as the warthog, which feed on both plants and animals. But the Serengeti is ruled by the great carnivores, lions and leopards. They hunt only infrequently as their needs require and spend days lolling about seemingly on holiday. Lesser meat-eaters, such as wild dogs and foxes prey on the smaller mammals, and lone hyenas scavenge the food that has been left behind by other carnivores.

The human role in the Serengeti is limited: Only sightseers and photographers are permitted there, along with the Masai, the proud, nomadic herders who have roamed the broad savanna with their cattle for centuries and are largely oblivious to the influence of modern culture.

*Serengeti National Park in north-central Tanzania is
the last great hope for many species of African
animals. In this 5,700-square-mile grassland,
animals roam free and protected.*

CHAPTER ELEVEN

*In a land that time seems to have forgotten, a
river, which is essential to the savanna ecosystem of
Tanzania, meanders along peacefully beneath
a pewter-colored sky.*

CHAPTER ELEVEN

*Timeless as the sea, grasses bristle in the wind on
the prairie that separates Australia's coastal areas
from the continent's harsh interior desert.*

CHAPTER ELEVEN

FRAGILE WETLANDS

Big Cypress Swamp sprawls across southwestern Florida. It is an inhospitable terrain of forbidding thickets and oppressive heat, which is about the size of the state of Delaware. The swamp is part of the same wetland system as the Florida Everglades, and water flowing out of the swamp nourishes the western side of the Everglades. But Big Cypress Swamp is higher and drier, and is its own unique ecological entity.

Almost nobody ventured into the swamp until about fifty years ago. Those who did brought back stories of huge alligators in awesome numbers, shoulder-deep muck, and swarms of insects too thick to see through. There were also huge stands of gigantic bald cypress trees, some eight feet thick, more than one hundred feet tall, and apparently, hundreds of years old. This all changed in the 1920s when the state highway department cut the Tamiami Trail through the heart of the swamp to carry motorists between Florida's two coasts. Since then the alligator population has been decimated, most of the cypress trees have been sawed down for timber, and large sections of the swamp have been drained for development.

A proposed airport on the eastern shore of Big Cypress Swamp brought matters to a head in 1968. Local communities envisioned an economic bonanza with new towns rising from drained swampland. Environmentalists were outraged. The water table had already dropped as much as ten feet because of land development, and the adjacent everglades were beginning to show signs of suffering from a water shortage. A battle between developers and environmentalists ensued, with both the White House and Congress intervening. Finally, in 1974 Congress voted to turn more than 500 thousand acres in the heart of Big Cypress into a national preserve at a cost of about $200 million for the purchase of land from private owners. Although western sections of the swamp have been damaged irrevocably by land development, the creation of the national preserve saved about forty percent of the original swamp.

A dense stand of fakahatchee pushes its way up
from the murky waters and deep muck of
Big Cypress Swamp adjacent to Everglades
National Park in Florida.

Big Cypress is a good place to see what environmental action can accomplish. If you go there, get out of your car along the Tamiami Trail. Stand beneath a dome of cypress trees, rich with hanging moss, vines, and orchids. If you feel bold, wade through one of the cool, pristine sloughs. Then stroll from the boggy cypress forest into a dryland area of tall grass dotted with islands of pine trees and cabbage palms. Elsewhere see hammocks of oak, bay, and mahogany. Look for animals. The vast swamp is a sanctuary for wildlife, and it is the last habitat for more than twenty rare or endangered species, including the Florida panther, Everglades mink, and wood stork.

The Big Cypress is a classic swamp: a body of water lying in a shallow depression with little drainage. Swamps usually develop in moist climates, often along low-lying coastal plains or in floodplains of rivers. The bottoms of swamps are usually near or below local water tables, so swamps often serve as runoffs for groundwater and help stabilize a region's water cycle. In the United States, there are an estimated hundred thousand square miles of swamps and other wetland. The largest expanses of wetland, such as the Big Cypress, occur along the warm and humid coastal plains of the Atlantic Ocean and the Gulf of Mexico.

A marsh is similar to a swamp, but its primary vegetation is low-lying grasses, rushes, and sedges. In Massachusetts swamplike wetlands are called fens, a word that may have been borrowed from the English. The Fens, a district of eastern England that was once the country's largest swampland, was originally drained by Romans and then drained again in the seventeenth century.

Bogs are a specialized kind of swamp that once appeared in great profusion in the middle-Atlantic states. Unfortunately, most bogs have been drained for farming. Bogs are ancient lake beds that gradually became overgrown with peat or sphagnum moss. They still exist in large numbers throughout Great Britain and Ireland, providing a habitat for such unique flora and fauna as the tiny bog turtle, a creature with a black sculptured shell and an orange head.

Wetlands provide food and shelter for birds, serve as nurseries for fish, and improve water quality for all life forms, including humans, by trapping sediments and removing pollution. All this makes them among the most productive ecosystems on earth.

Long strands of moss drip from the trees, almost touching the still water in Virginia Beach Swamp, a thriving wetland in a shallow depression with little drainage along the low-lying Atlantic coastal plain.

CHAPTER TWELVE

*This bog in Maine is alive with an astounding
variety of wetland plants that grow out of a
thick bed of sphagnum moss.*

CHAPTER TWELVE

*With just a short time to prosper during the
brief Alaskan summer, cranberries grow wild in
the marshy areas below the great peaks
in Denali National Park.*

CHAPTER TWELVE

195

The elements of a verdant Florida marsh are all here. There is still, warm water choked with floating plants, a rich variety of grasses, a few trees, and a broad blue sky.

REBUILDING WETLANDS

Is it possible for people to create a swamp or marsh that contains all the complexity of a natural wetland? Can people who for years have aggressively drained the swamps and filled in bogs restore these wondrous ecological systems to their full biological function as well as their aesthetic splendor?

In central Florida ecological engineers have attempted to restore an abandoned strip mine from a nearly lifeless wasteland into a living marsh. They used bulldozers to tear down an earthen dam that had controlled flooding and then graded the banks around the new marsh. Channels were dug to connect the marsh to a tidal creek, and a few nonnative plants were killed with herbicide.

After the bulldozers departed, the ecologists planted native grasses and trees from nurseries. Hard-to-get plants were removed from an established marsh and transferred to the new marsh, and salt hay and cordgrass were planted along the banks. By the time they were finished, the engineers had constructed a watery world of native plants that is a home to otters and alligators, and serves as a feeding ground for the glossy ibis and the endangered wood stork.

The new marsh appears vibrant now, but biologists believe it will have to be studied for years, perhaps decades, to determine whether it is biologically functional.

OPPOSITE
The wetland vegetation in Everglades National Park grows out of a thick layer of solidly packed muck, the rich, life-giving accumulation of millions of years of plant decay in warm, nearly stagnant water.

Red mangroves in West Lake in the Florida Everglades extend their long aerial roots deep into the mud. Their dense mass provides a safe home for countless tiny creatures.

RED MANGROVE

Where the Everglades meet the sea at the lower tip of the Florida peninsula, there is a primeval jungle cut into a maze of small islands by twisting channels of mucky water. Red mangrove trees tower as much as eight stories above the swampy water, which has been stained a dark rust color by tannin in the bark and leaves of the trees.

Up until the mid-1970s, people living in this area thought little of the red mangrove swamps. They were drained voraciously and replaced by housing developments, hotels, and shopping malls. But biologists from the University of Miami who were studying the swamps discovered that the little-loved mangrove tree was actually the basis of a subtle and elegant food chain, which sustained much of southern Florida's unique array of animal life.

What the biologists found was that red mangroves shed more than three tons of leaves per acre annually. Fungi and bacteria begin the organic breakdown of the fallen leaves. Decomposing leaves are eaten by microscopic crustaceans and worms whose excretions help to enrich the protein content of the organic matter. The tiny creatures in turn are eaten by small fish, which then become prey for larger fish, crustaceans, birds, and animals, and in some cases, eventually people.

The biologists also found that the red mangrove forests, which fringe the Pacific and Atlantic coastal areas of Central America and the Caribbean islands as well as southern Florida, also provide a safe wildlife habitat both on land and in the water around the roots. Mangroves break up waves and stabilize land vulnerable to erosion from the sea. Some people even believe these steamy mangrove forests offer the best refuge during a hurricane.

The roots of these mangrove trees stand firm against the tide, catching and holding silt and other material. In time, this buildup will be made fertile enough by decaying mangrove leaves to support other plants.

CHAPTER TWELVE

199

CHAPTER TWELVE

Although it is not actually a swamp but a very slow-moving river, the Everglades has a wetland ecosystem, anchored by expanses of saw grass broken here and there by clumps of pine trees.

CHAPTER TWELVE

*These reeds, catching the first glint of sunrise
on a Michigan lake, may be the harbingers of a
future marsh. As lake plants die and sink to
the bottom, they mix with sediment and
gradually fill in the lake.*

CHAPTER TWELVE

*This lake in Maine is well on its way to becoming a
swamp as it fills with decayed organic material.
It already boasts a myriad of plants that thrive
along its soggy shores.*

CHAPTER TWELVE

THE VAST OCEAN

Unceasing and timeless, wave and wind batter the crumbling cliffs of Cornwall into a wild and dangerous beauty. Ridges of broken black shale line the coves of this timeless land that is veiled in misty legends of pirates and King Arthur, and isolated from the rest of the world by its rugged terrain.

In 1916 novelist D.H. Lawrence described Cornwall's great black cliffs and rocks as primeval: "It is like the beginning of the world, wonderful, and so free and strong." Time has not diminished the romance of this magical place where sea and land converge to create a mystery that takes our breath and stirs our souls with the lure of the unknown. Land's End, a rocky headland that marks the western most point of England, lies at the very tip of Cornwall. Jagged piles of rock rise from the sea, wreathed in the spray of breaking waves. It is a savage scene both awesome and wonderful. Standing here facing out to the Atlantic Ocean as its embattled waters rage around the promontory, you feel drawn by the vast expanse of the sea.

It's only natural to feel the pull of the sea because our planet, Earth, is the water planet. A single vast ocean covers more than seventy percent of Earth's surface, broken here and there by the continental landmasses and the islands on which we live, always surrounded by water. The three great oceans of the world are the Pacific, the Atlantic, and the Indian, but if you turn a globe upside down, you will see that these oceans come together near the continent of Antarctica, forming what is sometimes called the Antarctic Ocean. The Atlantic and Pacific also meet at the top of the globe in the Arctic Ocean.

Scientists have been studying the oceans for about a century and still know very little about them. As more is known about the oceans, they are expected to become an even greater source of food for the planet's burgeoning billions, a new source of minerals, and even a source of energy. The world's first tidal power plant already uses the force of the endless tides to produce electricity in France.

By studying ocean temperatures, meteorologists also learn about the earth's climate. The seas control climate because water changes temperature more slowly than air or land and because the oceans cover so much of the earth's surface. This makes the oceans a steadying influence on land temperatures and also helps keep air temperature from becoming too hot or too cold for human habitation.

This rocky headland in Cornwall, known as Land's End, is the westernmost point of England, an island nation where the immense power of the sea is always close at hand.

How did the waters of the ocean come to cover such a vast area of our planet? Scientists are not yet sure, but one theory purports that water was trapped within rocks inside the earth as it formed. When the rocks cooled and became solid about five hundred million years ago, the water was released and filled the giant basins between the continents. Another leading theory maintains that seawater came from thick clouds that covered the earth during its formative period. As the earth cooled along with the clouds, rain poured forth for hundreds of years, filling the planet's great basins.

In either case, scientists are certain that the same water molecules have been cycling for millions of years as the waters of the ocean mix with each other, then evaporate to form clouds and fall as freshwater on land and sea. It is estimated that one molecule of water circulates through the world's oceans every five thousand years. If the molecule escapes into the hydrologic cycle and begins circling through the atmosphere, it may travel around the world every five hundred years. Every time you take a swallow of water, you take in millions and millions of these molecules. Because of this ongoing circulation of water over the centuries, it is probable that at least one molecule in your last glass of water was once drunk by Cleopatra.

Wherever sea and land converge—whether on flat coastal plains, like most of America's eastern seaboard, or where great mountains fall down to the water, such as Yugoslavia's spectacular Adriatic coast—people seem to gather. Some settle permanently; others come just to have a look. Almost everybody has his or her favorite coast: southern England and Land's End; the dark, forbidding cliffs of Scotland; South Africa's western coast that is rich in colors not seen elsewhere; or a remote beach on any tropical island.

Every shoreline is an ongoing struggle between sea and land. The relentless pounding of the sea and the wind brings constant change. Over time gentle slopes become cliffs, cliffs become steeper, and beaches disappear. Where large waves break offshore, a sandbar forms. Smaller waves build a lower bar near shore. A lagoon forms after waves build a sandbar above the waterline. Waves wash sand into the lagoon, and the lagoon becomes a marsh and eventually a region of sand dunes.

Never the same twice, waves wash ashore on a sandy beach. Scientists believe that a single water molecule will take about five thousand years to make a circuit through the world's oceans.

CHAPTER THIRTEEN

The Twelve Apostles are giant rock formations on the southern coast of Victoria, Australia. They were once part of the continent until the intervening rock was washed away by the relentless power of the sea.

Polished by the churning water of the sea, rocks sprawl across a beach along this section of the Maine coast, which many people feel is the loveliest and most romantic shoreline anywhere.

CHAPTER THIRTEEN

The skeletal remains of stony corals create massive limestone formations that provide a safe haven for living corals and an incredible array of marine life.

OPPOSITE
One of the world's wonders, Great Barrier Reef, is a natural breakwater for the northeastern coast of Australia. The largest coral reef in the world extends for 1,250 miles and is a haven for hundreds of species of brightly colored fish.

GREAT BARRIER REEF

One of nature's most extraordinary creations, Great Barrier Reef extends for over 1,200 miles off the northeast coast of Australia. Made up almost entirely of living coral, the reef and the many islands it has spawned are a glittering string of jewels shining in bright tropical waters 15 to 150 miles offshore.

Between reef and shore, a vast lagoon is strewn with hilly, often forested continental islands (the exposed peaks of mountains that were once part of Australia). It has more than ninety flat coral cays along with countless islets, named and unnamed, made of living coral and often buried by the tides.

This enchanting wonderland consists of gardens of coral, usually just a few feet below the surface, that are dappled by sunlight and thronged with fish of every color in an unbelievable kaleidoscope of shapes, sizes, and hues. The reef boasts an estimated eleven hundred species of fish. Clusters of coral, tinged bright red, golden yellow, and iridescent blue, resemble perfectly arranged bouquets of flowers. In deeper waters, large round boulders of coral rise up from the depths of the Pacific Ocean. Some are monoliths that are more than two thousand years old.

Thickets of multibranched staghorn coral, colored beige or sometimes blue from algae, are hidden in sheltered valleys and on ledges along the reef. Elsewhere, groves of round plate coral rise on slender stems like mushrooms.

*At the far eastern end of Long Island, New York,
waves cut away the Montauk coast, working
steadily to create a delightful wide sandy beach.*

*Bleak in winter and shimmering in summer, the
coast of Maine is famous for its rugged beauty that
is a unique blend of rocks, trees, and waves.*

THE VAST OCEAN

CHAPTER THIRTEEN

213

Chesapeake Bay is fed by the Susquehanna, Potomac, Rappahannock, and James rivers, which bring in a mixed bag of industrial and agricultural pollutants along with life-giving freshwater.

LIFE IN AN ESTUARY

Romantic, historic Chesapeake Bay is a vast inlet of the Atlantic Ocean that is larger than the state of Delaware. It extends inland more than three hundred miles from its mouth in southern Virginia. Called a drowned-mouth estuary, the bay was formed when the mouth of the Susquehanna River was covered during the rising of the oceans following the melting of the Pleistocene ice sheets about ten thousand years ago.

An estuary is a partially enclosed coastal bay or inlet where freshwater mixes with water from the sea. Chesapeake and most other estuaries are one of the most sensitive and ecologically important habitats on earth. Like other estuaries, including San Francisco Bay, Chesapeake is lined with salt marshes and lagoons that provide sanctuary for many unique species of waterfowl, specialized fish, and other sea creatures, including the culinary favorite Chesapeake crabs. Among its significant ecological functions, Chesapeake Bay stores nutrients for larval and juvenile marine life, and serves as a breeding area for many species of ocean fish.

Unfortunately, Chesapeake Bay lies near the major population centers of Baltimore and Washington, D.C., and has been severely challenged by civilization. Tidal land has been reclaimed, swamps and marshes have been filled, and the water of the bay has been polluted with sewage as well as solid and industrial wastes. Sediments have begun to change the salinity of the bay. All these factors have begun to take their toll on the plant and animal life of the bay. Fortunately, the federal government has stepped in to help save the Chesapeake's unique environment.

In Chesapeake Bay, a fascinating estuary near Washington, D.C., sea and freshwater mix to create a unique natural environment that is rich in oysters, crabs, and other marine life.

CHAPTER THIRTEEN

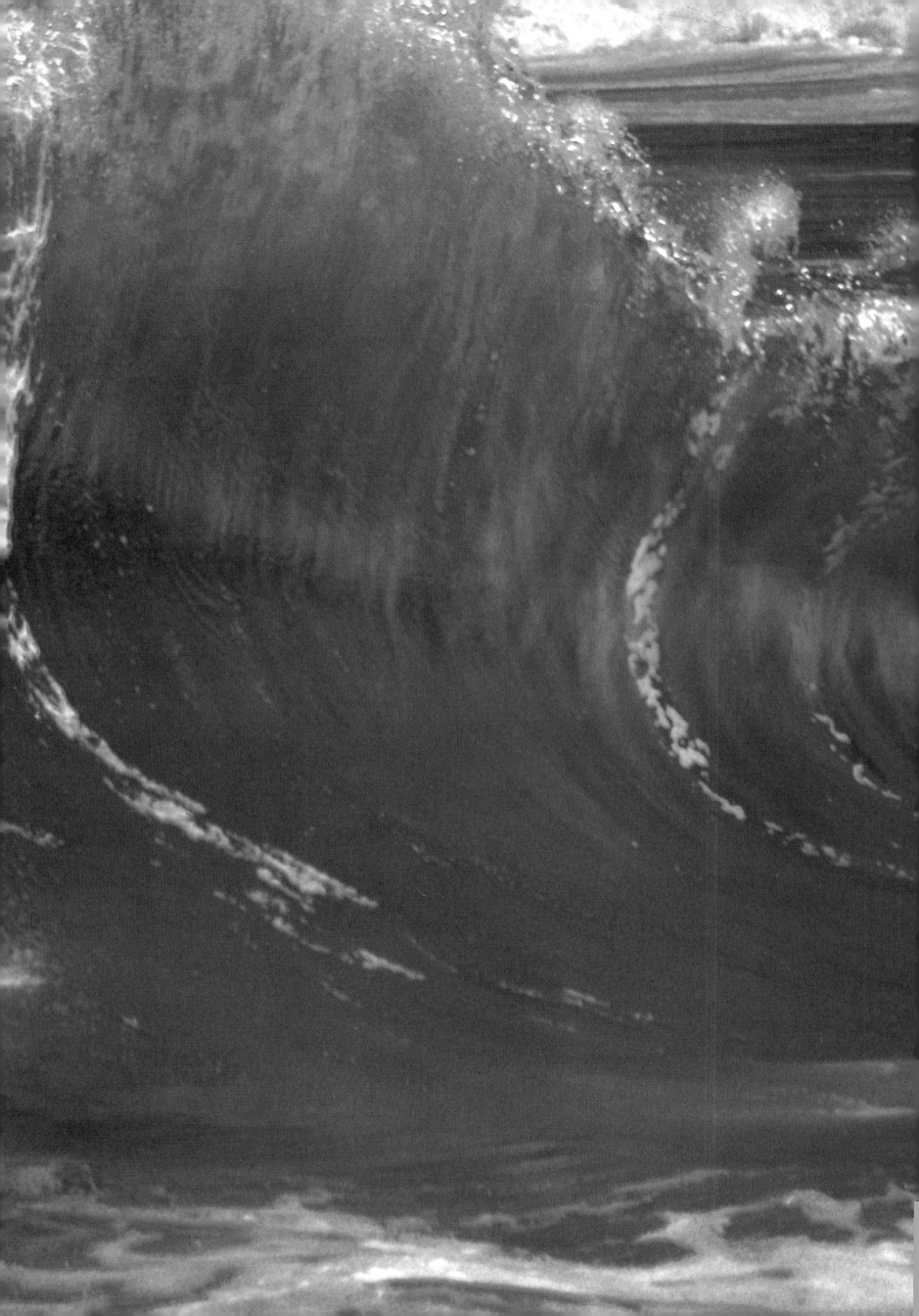

Big Sur is a stunningly beautiful stretch of California coast south of the Monterey Peninsula, where mountains of the Santa Lucia Range meet the Pacific Ocean head on.

The constant pounding of waves against rock eventually creates a sandy beach where once there may have been high cliffs. On this Atlantic beach, sea oats valiantly hold the dunes against the wind.

PRECEDING PAGES
When this wave rolls in from its long journey across the open ocean, it will pound the shoreline with the force of about two tons to the square foot.

CHAPTER THIRTEEN

ISLAND WORLDS

Dramatically beautiful, with four simmering volcanoes rising up from lush rice paddies and stunning white beaches, Bali defines what a tropical island should be. Just a dot on the world map, Bali is only slightly larger than the state of Delaware. It lies eight degrees south of the equator in the sweeping archipelago that constitutes the Republic of Indonesia. Bali is a dreamland of golden sunsets and lush green landscapes that draws countless visitors to its shores each year. In the 1930s when Indonesia was still a Dutch colony, writers, artists, and anthropologists, who were transfixed by its idyllic villages where religious pageantry is a daily occurrence, made Bali famous.

A constant visual delight, Bali beguiles visitors with rain forests, misty lakes, hilly scrubland, and endless rice terraces thick with chartreuse wands of rice. The higher you go into the mountains, the more Bali unfolds, layer by layer. The Balinese, whose religion is a combination of Hinduism and animism, have built small shrines and temples everywhere. There they stage religious festivals and make elaborate offerings. Not a seafaring people, they believe that demons haunt the sea. Most Balinese people farm for a living and believe their homeland is a divine property leased from the gods.

No one has ever been able to count all the islands on earth. According to geographers and geologists, an island is any area of land surrounded entirely by water. Because the world's oceans are a continuous body of water, all the continents would seem to be islands. On the globe, Antarctica and Australia certainly look just like large islands. But geologists say they aren't: The largest island is Greenland, followed in order of size by New Guinea, Borneo, Madagascar, Baffin Island, Sumatra, Honshu (Japan's largest island), and Great Britain. At the other end of the scale are tiny islets, some scarcely bigger than a big rock sticking out of the sea.

A constant visual delight, lush Bali is a small but densely populated island, where the people's careful respect for natural resources has created this beautiful and highly efficient style of farming, rice terraces.

Geologists classify Bali as an oceanic island—the result of a volcanic eruption far from a major landmass. The most remote island in the world is also an oceanic island: little, uninhabited Bouvet in the South Atlantic. The other category of earth's islands is continental. These islands were once part of neighboring continents. Continental islands were formed when an isthmus or part of a peninsula was covered with water. Great Britain was once a coastal highland that became isolated from Europe when rising ocean waters submerged the lowest parts of the land. Japan, Sicily, Newfoundland, Sri Lanka, and Manhattan also used to be part of larger landmasses.

Although there are similarities, no island formed in exactly the same way as any other. Its formation may be the result of plate tectonics, the slow but awesome movement of the enormous plates on the earth's crust that float upon denser, hotter material below. These titanic movements broke off enormous islands, such as Madagascar, from continental rims and uplifted other islands, such as Japan, along the edges of the plates.

As oceanic plates glide over an especially hot spot in the underlying layer, molten rock can push up a string of volcanic islands far from shore. This is the way the Hawaiian group and the Galapagos were formed. Another volcanic island, Iceland, formed when two great plates pulled apart, releasing magma from below. In tropical regions, a volcanic island often erodes as colonies of coral build upon its offshore debris and grow toward sunlight, forming a reef. Eventually, the volcano disappears completely, leaving only a coral atoll surrounding a lagoon.

Just as the geography of each island is unique, so are the people, animals, and plants that inhabit them. No island is the same as any other: think of Easter Island, with its brooding stone statues; bustling Hong Kong, an island of commerce; remote and volcanic Iceland; green, cultivated Ireland; beautiful, wild New Zealand; manic Manhattan; the prison island of Alcatraz; proper Great Britain; and frozen, frigid Greenland. The inhabitants of an island seem to be molded by their island, whether it is a tropical paradise or a rocky, storm-battered outpost in a high latitude. People feel protected on their island, with its immutable natural frontiers. The island gives people a sharp sense of identity and sometimes a belief that they belong to a chosen race. Maybe this is why people born and bred on large continents, crisscrossed by international boundaries, like to visit islands: for a while they too can feel special.

Iceland is a verdant oceanic island, formed by ongoing volcanic action, that is considered to be a part of Europe. The landscape here is punctuated by steaming geysers and fumaroles.

CHAPTER FOURTEEN

*Made unusually fertile by rich volcanic ash, the
topsoil of Waipio Valley on the island of Hawaii
supports a startling array of plant life that thrives
year round in the tropical climate.*

*A rocky headland greets the sea in Hawaii, a group
of exquisitely beautiful islands created by volcanoes
rising from the floor of the Pacific Ocean that have
been worn away by wind and rain.*

CHAPTER FOURTEEN

*Mount Agung is one of four active volcanoes
on Bali, a small island in the Indonesian
archipelago that has an international reputation
for golden sunsets.*

CHAPTER FOURTEEN

*Stirring the imagination, the coastline of Kauai in
Hawaii is a magnificent meeting place of the blue
sea and sky with the green tropical vegetation.*

CHAPTER FOURTEEN

*The Seychelles are an unusual group of a hundred
islands in the Indian Ocean, with boulders the
size of houses balanced in impossible ways and
gigantic stone monoliths rising like toadstools
above rain forests.*

OPPOSITE
*Gleaming white beaches line the mythical Seychelles,
a group of islands spread across the Indian Ocean
in an area that is about the same size as the
state of California.*

MAGICAL SEYCHELLES

A hundred islands splashed across the Indian
Ocean a thousand miles off the coast of Kenya, the
Seychelles are so different from most other islands that
visitors find them magical and otherworldly. Unlike
other oceanic islands, they are made of granite piled
into steep, dark mountains that have been eroded and
furrowed into gigantic forms. The outer Seychelles are
geologically young coral atolls and cays, but the
ancient islands in the center, including the main island
of Mahé, consist of granite that is about 650 million
years old. Scientists are uncertain about the origin of
the Seychelles, but there are several theories. They may
be a fragment of the continent that was left behind
when India broke away from Africa 135 million years
ago. Or the Seychelles may once have been part of
Africa's east coast.

Most of the Seychelles are covered with tropical
rain forests that contain species found nowhere else on
earth: jellyfish trees, vanilla orchids, giant coco-de-mer
plants, black parrots, and blue pigeons. No ancient
people inhabited the Seychelles. If they had, surely they
would have created myths about this strange and
beguiling place. Its mountains, unbelievable rock formations, boulders the size of houses balanced in impossible ways, and gigantic monoliths rising like toadstools above the thick rain forest seem to be more
fanciful than real.

People have come to the Seychelles only recently.
French settlers arrived at the end of the eighteenth
century. Later, the British governed until the islands
achieved independence in 1976. Today, most of the
people arriving in this mystical island world are
tourists from Europe and Australia.

CHAPTER FOURTEEN

*Glacial ice created this U-shaped fjord in
Prince Christian Sound, Greenland. Except for
a relatively narrow strip of coastline, the world's
largest island is covered by an ice sheet fourteen
thousand feet thick.*

CHAPTER FOURTEEN

Looking very different from a tropical island, the Cotswalds is a peaceful rural area in central England, part of the British Isles off the northwestern coast of Europe.

CHAPTER FOURTEEN

231

Looking as though it has put on a string of pearls,
Bora-Bora, a volcanic island in the South Pacific,
is surrounded by a protective lagoon created by
the buildup of coral.

PRECEDING PAGES
Almost everybody is drawn to a tropical beach,
where the waves roll in endlessly, the sun shines
every day, and time seems to stand still.

CHAPTER FOURTEEN

Pinnacle Rock on Bartolume Island is one of many unusual landforms in the mysterious Galapagos Islands, a natural zoo, isolated from the rest of the world, where wildlife found nowhere else prospers.

CHAPTER FOURTEEN

EARTH AND SKY

At dusk in the tropical paradise of Tahiti, the sun seems to set in the palm of your hand. In Montana the colors of the setting sun fill the sky, while in New England the sun often seems to sneak away with little fanfare. In northern California in the day's final moment, the sun seems to plunge into the sea, sometimes offering a quick green flash as an afterthought. Sunsets in Key West, Florida, are so dramatic that almost every evening crowds of acrobats, musicians, street vendors, and tourists gather on a pier to celebrate them. In Iceland in winter, the sun's fierce fire looks distant and cold as it drops into the North Atlantic Ocean at the end of a brief arctic day.

Everywhere on earth, there is magic and mystery in the instant the sun disappears from view, turning day into night. The moment is such an absolute demarcation of time that most ancient people considered one day to end and the next to begin at sunset. When the sun drops below the horizon, some people's imaginations are fired by the lure of distant lands still basking in its glow. Others simply glory in the colors, reds, oranges, and yellows, that last little more than an instant.

In the glorious moment of sunset, our attention is riveted to the horizon, but this visual margin is a constant in everyone's life, a reference point for each of us. Our imagination is drawn to the place where mountains touch the sky, where the sky meets the sea, where the known ends and the unknown begins. In an earlier age of exploration, the endlessly receding horizon drew Magellan and other seafarers around the earth. Later, it pulled the American pioneers west. Sometimes distant and sometimes near, no matter how far you travel toward it, the horizon always separates the familiar from the new, dividing one world from the next.

The common component of any horizon anywhere is the sky. From the beginning of history, people have looked up to the sky and marveled. High overhead, the sun, moon, and stars gave us the means to reckon time in days, months, and years. In ancient times the sky became a powerful symbol, the place where the gods dwelled, controlling weather, the seasons, and other events on earth. In the Christian epistemology it is the place where people go for an eternally blissful afterlife, following a lifetime of toil and trouble on earth.

There is hardly anything on earth more magical
than a sunset viewed through the branches of
a palm tree on the island of Hawaii.

CHAPTER FIFTEEN

The sky, never still and always moving, brings life to earth. The invisible wind, which is the movement of the molecules of oxygen, nitrogen, and the other gases that make up our atmosphere, creates the weather. Rain-bearing clouds form when rising warm air collides with descending cold air. Where the leading edge of one air mass collides with another, thunder and lightning can result from the ensuing friction in just the same way that your feet pick up static electricity when you shuffle across a carpet.

Hawks and eagles ride the thermal currents created by the rising warm air, and the wind works as the go-between in the pollination of plants. Aspen trees produce catkins to be carried aloft, while maples launch seeds that look like little helicopters as they spin and fall through the sky. Other plants, such as dandelions and milkweed, send forth seeds that resemble little parachutes riding the wind.

Why is the sky blue? This question has worried many philosophers and scientists, including Aristotle and Leonardo da Vinci. Isaac Newton, one of the greatest scientific thinkers of all time, finally provided the answer: Light from the sun is really a spectrum of many different colored rays, all adding up to what looks like pure white light. Different colors of light from the sun are selectively scattered by minute particles of dust and vapor floating in the earth's atmosphere.

When the sun is overhead during the day, the rays of light with long wave lengths, including red and orange, pass through the atmosphere, while blue light, which has a shorter wave length, is scattered by these particles. If there is a large amount of dust or pollution in the air, more and more colors are scattered and the sky becomes whitish or hazy. The sky is bluest in winter, when the air is less humid. It is also especially blue after a rain storm, high on a mountain, or at sea.

As night falls, one side of the earth turns away from the sun, and the sun's light must travel farther than when the sun is overhead. At this time the blue rays that are traveling tangentially to the surface of the earth are scattered even more than during the day. The longer red and orange rays also begin to scatter as the sun nears the horizon. The result can be a spectacular red sunset that becomes even more spectacular if there is an array of clouds overhead to reflect the final light from the sun. Once the sun has disappeared below the horizon, sometimes there is a short burst of green light because green is the last color of the sun's spectrum to zip through the atmosphere.

Dancing in the light, cumulus clouds reflect the colors of the spectrum that occurs in rays of light from the sun.

CHAPTER FIFTEEN

*Saguaro cacti in the Sonora Desert await the passing
of the day under a sky rich with the many colors of
an Arizona sunset.*

*The bands of intense color in this magnificent
desert sunset are created as light from the moving
sun strikes particles of dust and other debris
in the atmosphere.*

*Calling children to come trick or treat, a big yellow
moon appears low in the evening sky when the light
from the moon passes through the large volume of
atmosphere near the horizon.*

*Washing the sky with rich, deep colors, a sunset
over the ocean creates a magical horizon that
encourages you to dream of distant lands.*

*This display of one of nature's most awesome
and dangerous powers, a bolt of lightning, rips
through the sky above the broad open plains
near Laramie, Wyoming.*

*In this rainstorm at sea, you can almost see the
hydrologic cycle lifting briny seawater through
evaporation into the atmosphere and returning it
to earth as refreshing rain.*

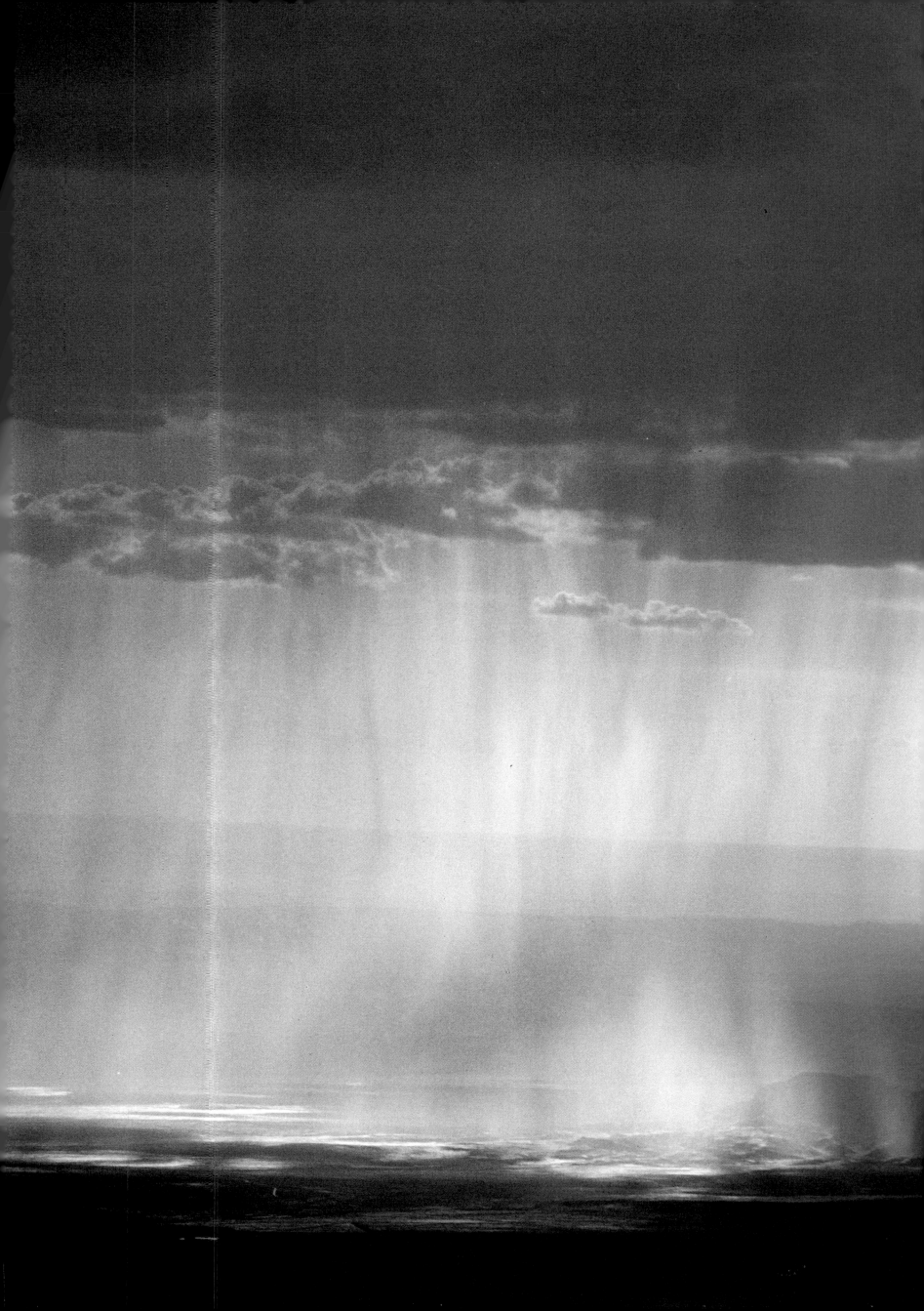

Among the most magnificent of all natural phenomenon, the northern lights, or aurora borealis, work their magic in Denali National Park, Alaska.

NORTHERN LIGHTS SOUTHERN LIGHTS

The land of the midnight sun is a land of extremes. Days go from 24 hours of constant daylight to 24 hours of darkness at the Arctic Circle (66 degrees 31 minutes north latitude). At the North Pole, there are six months of daylight followed by six months of darkness. No matter the season, the sun always lies at a low angle above the horizon, creating spectacular sunsets that can last for hours.

The endless nights can be as stunning as the long sunsets because a wondrous, luminous display of light and color may fill the sky. Among the most magnificent of all natural phenomena, the northern lights glow in brilliant reds, yellows, greens, blues, and violets. The lights are arrayed in a multitude of shapes, including arcs, streamers, rays, great hanging tapestries, and drapes. The farther north you go, the brighter the lights and the more fantastic the shapes.

Also called the aurora borealis, this natural light show occurs between 35 and 600 miles above the earth. It seems to coincide with periods of great sunspot activity, and scientists believe it is caused by high-speed electrons and protons from the sun that have become trapped in the Van Allen radiation belt far above earth. From there, these particles are drawn to the earth's poles by the powerful polar magnetic fields.

The best place to see the show is along a line extending from northern Norway across Hudson Bay and through northern Alaska to Siberia. The equally brilliant display centering on the South Pole is called the aurora australis, or the southern lights.

OPPOSITE
The eerie light of the aurora borealis is believed to be caused by high-speed electrons and protons from the sun that have become trapped in the Van Allen radiation belt far above earth.

CHAPTER FIFTEEN

250

Caused by the interaction of static electricity in the atmosphere and colliding masses of air, lightning creates an alien landscape in clouds at night.

The day that is dawning on this lake is unlikely to be fair. The mackerel sky (cirrocumulus clouds) and red dawn warn sailors and fishermen that a storm system is developing.

PRECEDING PAGES
As the day comes to an end, the sun seems to plunge directly into the sea off the California coast.

CHAPTER FIFTEEN

*These swirling wheels of light around the Pole Star,
which gets its name from being directly above the
North Pole, are striking evidence of the rotation
of the earth around its axis.*

*A symbol of hope and a promise of fair weather, a
rainbow is created when a large number of water
molecules in the atmosphere refract and reflect all
the colors in the spectrum of sunlight.*

CHAPTER FIFTEEN

CHAPTER FIFTEEN

These billowing cumulus clouds forecast fair weather. The strong contrasts in color are not caused by threatening rain but are shadows cast by the part of the cloud nearest the sun.

Puffs of light and dark clouds froth up along a front where a high-pressure system has encountered a system of low-pressure air.

*Shining through a tree, the full moon casts an eerie
glow. The moon's irregular cycles do not coincide
with the earth's annual trip around the sun—a fact
that confounded some ancient astronomers.*

CHAPTER FIFTEEN